Lost Restaurants

of

CHARLESTON

·········· JESSICA SURFACE

AMERICAN PALATE

Published by American Palate
A Division of The History Press
Charleston, SC
www.historypress.com

Copyright © 2019 by Jessica Surface
All rights reserved

First published 2019

Manufactured in the United States

ISBN 9781467142298

Library of Congress Control Number: 2019948145

Contents

Acknowledgements

A special thank-you is owed to the many restaurant owners, family members, current and former employees and historians who took the time to share their stories and memories with me. The guidance and wealth of knowledge from the staff and archives at the Charleston Museum, Historic Charleston Foundation, South Carolina Historical Society, and Charleston County Public Library was also incredibly helpful on this journey. To my husband, Reid, a big thank you for your help in researching, reading, rereading and cheerleading throughout this process. It's been more than fifteen years since freshman chemistry class, and you continue to be the best library partner a girl could ask for.

Introduction

W hat's your favorite restaurant in town?" is the most difficult—and frequently asked—question I receive as a food tour guide in Charleston. While it seems like such a simple inquiry, I promise there's no easy answer. In fact, I would dare to venture that if you ask any local for their personal favorite, you'll receive no less than three answers.

The sheer volume of options certainly plays a part in this quandary, but to be honest, Charleston's rocket to international culinary fame has left us all a bit spoiled. (Seriously, when did I become the person who refuses to order a Moscow Mule unless the ginger beer is housemade?) So, in the quest to appropriately answer the question, I often require a few clarifying follow ups: You mean my favorite casual lunch? How about a fancy, no-price-limit dinner? What about breakfast food at eleven at night? I have favorites for each of those. Does the place need to be haunted, historic or a film site for the television show *Southern Charm*? I can recommend seven options for each.

It should come as no surprise that when I sat down to write about the lost restaurants of Charleston, the available choices were overwhelming. The pages that follow are the result of a working list whittled down from a few hundred establishments in the beginning of the research process. In fact, for a short while I had to refrain from telling people about this project because the suggestion pile was more than overflowing.

For the selfish sake of my own sanity, the stories in this book are exclusive to restaurants that originated on the peninsula in downtown Charleston. The story expands from there, of course, out to West Ashley, Folly Beach, Mount Pleasant and beyond, but it was necessary to hone the focus over more than three hundred years of restaurants.

This is my guarded way of acknowledging that there will be some beloved restaurants that just aren't included in this collection. In fact, many that I miss. I made new friends over the fried jasmine rice balls and glasses of "bubbles" at Social, experienced the apocalyptic party mentality on the last night of the Blind Tiger I used to know and waited what seemed like decades for Parlor Deluxe to open so they could take my money in exchange for gourmet waffles and hot dogs, only to lose them just a short while later. But alas, those are my own experiences, a testament to the unique bonds we form with a location. Our favorite memories tied with favorite foods; that feeling of being happy, content and full.

Since restaurants create this connection beyond their obvious purpose, when one closes, it means a whole lot more to the rest of us than a simple business transaction. And if there's one thing I know about Charleston, it's that its people wish things could stay the same. Don't mess with our regular lunch spots and our anniversary restaurants and, for crying out loud, don't turn any of them into another hotel.

Regardless of the path to get here, this research process allowed me the opportunity to live for a moment in the different versions of this city that so many people reminisce about: the "old" Henry's, the crushed velvet of Perdita's, Robert belting out an aria while escorting a Chateaubriand around a dining room. There's a responsibility to each of these establishments, their owners and the people who created fond memories there.

So, with that sense of connection and respect, I am honored to share the stories of some of the lost restaurants of Charleston.

1
Charleston's Restaurant Beginnings

Charleston has earned an impressive reputation as a destination city. We have beautiful architecture, historical sightseeing and sunny beaches. If you're lucky, you can even spot Bill Murray here from time to time. But it's unlikely that you'll talk to anyone about Charleston without mentioning the food or our reputation for culinary excellence. And since we are able to trace our roots way, way back, it's not surprising that evidence remains of some of the very first lost restaurants.

Taverns were established in Charleston very early on, but they offered more than just a shot of your favorite spirit. Sure, guests could grab a drink or a meal, but they would also sit and open their mail, have a meeting with colleagues or just take care of their day-to-day business. Sound a bit like modern coffee shops where people make themselves at home? Well, we had those too. Coffeehouses were already popular in England, and the first one in Charleston was opened at the corner of Church and Queen Streets in 1724.[1] However, when those English taverns began to be replaced by French coffeehouses in the late 1700s, a bit of a rivalry ensued.

Taverns attempted to advertise potentially harmful effects of coffee while hyping the benefits of their distilled inventory. Coffeehouses took a different approach by promoting coffee drinking as an act of refinement and class. Quite frankly, it's difficult to choose a side in that equally convincing battle, but when taverns began losing too much money, many just converted into coffeehouses. Even the famous McCrady's Tavern, where George Washington visited in 1791, became the French Coffee House in the 1800s.[2]

These establishments were the backdrops of many important moments in Charleston's history, and the Carolina Coffee House was one prime example. Located at Tradd Street and Bedon's Alley, Vice President Aaron Burr happened to dine at this particular establishment in May 1802, just a few short years before his infamous duel with Alexander Hamilton. The citizens in attendance were clearly honored by their prestigious guest that night, considering the dinner provided in his honor included a whopping seventeen different toasts.[3]

Perhaps coffeehouses could even be considered the incubators for Charleston's early hospitality industry. They may have served coffee for a few cents, but they also offered a daily ordinary for dinner; staged entertainment, such as concerts and balls; sold tickets to events around town; and hosted meetings for important society organizations. Many of these establishments eventually went on to become inns or hotels, as well. Coffeehouses were essentially the meeting places around town, and as one article stated in 1956, "A man was better known for his coffee house than his home."[4]

Remy Mignot was a local businessman who knew the true value of these coffeehouses. While he already owned the Cheap Confectionary store at Meeting and Pinckney Streets, he purchased the United States Coffee House in 1837 with two partners: Alexis Gallot and French chef Louis Lefeve. They expanded the original business site, stating they would "supply their Larder with all that is rare and delicious, in Fish, Flesh, and Fowl, no expense or exertion will be spared."[5]

These partners quickly helped to up the ante in coffeehouse fare, even advertising exotic Parisian- and New York–style restaurants. A positive review raving about the waiters, accommodations and daily ordinary appeared in the paper shortly after the opening.[6]

While these taverns and coffeehouses offered a place for community, the focus of fine dining in the early nineteenth century was very different from what we know today. It wasn't all about scoring the finest restaurant reservations, but rather it was about securing a spot at the most exclusive society dinners and banquets. These large social gatherings would often need to be catered since they were held away from conventional kitchens in large public spaces.

This unique set of culinary hurdles presented the opportunity to separate amateur caterers from true professionals. If caterers could keep hot dishes hot and cold dishes cold, supply the best-looking table settings or secure hard-to-find ingredients, they would earn high respect for their craft. These heroes of the time provided mobile comfort—something people might not be able to fully appreciate until they've sweated their way through any Charleston social event in the summer.

In the 1800s, these caterers were mostly free black men and women, many of whom had a powerful and unique impact on the beginnings of Charleston's culinary scene. In fact, the title of pastry chef was one of the most distinguished positions among slaves at the time, and many of the best home cooks were trained by free black pastry chefs.[7]

While there were many important contributors during this time period, one notable name in Charleston's culinary history was Nat Fuller. He had already established himself as one of the city's best caterers and had even catered such large and important events as the Carolina Jockey Club Ball. So, what else was left for him to try? In 1860, Fuller decided to open his own restaurant, the Bachelor's Retreat, at 77 Church Street. The location was a success and became a regular meeting place for local societies.

One advertised dinner in 1862 demonstrated Fuller's impressive ability to procure a wide variety of meats, including a rare lamb mutton, ham, oysters, calf head soup, chicken pies, ducks and boned turkey.[8] And, of course, Fuller often served up the elusive and luxurious turtle soup that was quite the treat at the time. While sickness and the perils of the Civil War caused Nat Fuller to move his business around town, he remained well connected in his offerings to the public, even during the blockades of the Civil War.

Fuller's legacy as a caterer in Charleston was remembered at the Nat Fuller Feast, which was held in April 2015 in the historic Long Room of McCrady's Restaurant. The meal was an opportunity to re-create his famous "miscegenation dinner" that celebrated the end of the Civil War by bringing together both black and white citizens in 1865.

David S. Shields did a tremendous amount of research on these early caterers and restaurateurs for his book, *Southern Provisions: The Creation and Revival of a Cuisine*. His research helps highlight the importance of these early influencers and is highly recommended for a deeper look at the accomplishments of these individual artists. After all, these first lost restaurants helped set the scene for what was to come in Charleston.

Our story picks up at the turn of the twentieth century in Charleston, specifically with the South Carolina Inter-State and West Indian Exposition in 1901. In 1895, Atlanta had held its successful Cotton States Exposition, and businessmen in Charleston felt the city could benefit from a similar sort of fair. While it could have been interpreted as shameless self-promotion, many people could see the opportunity as a smart business move to increase trade and thrust Charleston into the spotlight. It was all a far cry from the highly publicized status Charleston enjoys with much less effort today.

In the official guide for the exposition, the organizers explained their objectives in greater detail:

> *This Exposition is held to inaugurate new industries and commerce in the South; to open up new foreign markets, particularly in the West Indies; to begin the Twentieth Century of the Christian era with an exhibition of the arts and peace; to develop the American culture of silk and tea; to promote the Southern manufactures of cotton and iron; to establish new steamship lines from Charleston, the central seaport of the Great Southeast; to show the world the resources and attractions of the territory along the Southern Seaboard, and the advantages of Charleston as a connecting link between the producers of the Southeastern States and the Mississippi Valley, on one side and the markets of the world on the other.*[9]

The South Carolina Inter-State and West Indian Exposition created the opportunity for new restaurants in Charleston. *From South Carolina Inter-State and West Indian Exposition Official Guide, 1901.*

While the organizers were aware that the exposition in Charleston wouldn't be as large as the Chicago World's Fair that was held in 1893, they still had incredibly high hopes, stating, "It will contribute as much, or more, to the expansion of American commerce and the peace of the world."[10] They dedicated two hundred acres of land for the exposition—a space that is now home to Hampton Park and the Citadel—which was lavishly built up and landscaped.

The exposition ran from December 1, 1901, to June 1, 1902, and like any giant undertaking with nearly impossible expectations, it might not have gone off exactly how they imagined. Sure, the weather wasn't great, and they didn't see the number of people or make the amount of money they were hoping for, but Charleston did end up with a long-standing restaurant.

OLYMPIA CAFE

The Olympia Cafe was meant to be a temporary establishment to serve the grand influx of people who were expected to arrive for the exposition, but it ended up as one of the longest-running restaurants in the city. The first location was at the northwest corner of King and Columbus Streets, just a block south of Line Street. This intersection is still considered to be fairly north on the peninsula, but this area was important at the time due to its proximity to the railway centers, including Union Station, which was built in 1907.

A small, one-story building with a long marble countertop, the cafe was smack dab in between the business and transportation centers of the city. That meant it often served railroad workers and citizens coming to and from Union Station in the heyday of railroad travel. Anyone could grab a bite to

Union Station was a busy railway hub at East Bay and Columbus Streets in the early twentieth century. *From Library of Congress Prints & Photographs Division, Detroit Publishing Company Collection.*

eat between their trains or before sightseeing in the area. To accommodate the train schedules, the building was open day and night and was often the busiest with the nocturnal crowd.

Unfortunately, the original building had to be destroyed in 1939 to make way for a service station on the lot. But that wasn't the end of the Olympia Cafe—it would simply be relocated directly across the street. Demos Pappas, who owned the business with his partner, Charles Costopulos, said of the new location, "A corner is always a corner, but I guess our old customers will find us in the new place."[11]

That new place was located at 621 King Street, and the customers did indeed find them there. In 1944, as their success continued, the partners were eventually able to buy the building for $12,500 from the estate of Mary Jane Ross.[12] The cafe also continued its reputation for reliable food and service. The menu didn't offer anything too fancy, instead it was the kind of place for a reasonable meal and cup of coffee. It was also the home of some of the best beef stew in Charleston. Serving up hearty dishes, Olympia Cafe had the intention of filling up hardworking railway workers and truck drivers. And those working men came in almost every day—the kind of familiar faces that didn't even need to put an order in for "the usual."

Demos became the sole proprietor of the café in 1947 and ran the place until his retirement in 1964. He had to be proud of his restaurant, which was one of the oldest in the city and in operation for an impressive sixty-two years. A quote about his retirement in the paper read, "Life is just too short, its owner figured, to cope with a bewildering morass of federal regulations. Not while there's plenty of time left to just take it easy."[13]

DEMOS RESTAURANT

While the railways were bustling in the north of the peninsula, the business district was in full force on Broad Street. In fact, the building at the northwest corner of Broad and East Bay was once home to many different businesses. Dating as far back as 1778, the building was once home to an apothecary and hosted experiments with laughing gas before it evolved into the Bank of South Carolina and eventually became the J.S. Pinkussohn Cigar Company.[14] When Arthur L. Moore purchased the store in December 1915, he added a soda fountain and dairy lunch service to the existing establishment.

Above: Demos Restaurant was located at the corner of Broad and East Bay Streets. *From Library of Congress Prints & Photographs Division, Detroit Publishing Company Collection.*

Left: The Demos Brothers' dairy lunch was popular in the city's business district. *From Walsh's Charleston City Directory, 1919.*

MADE IN U.S.A.
WADSWORTH, OHIO
THE OHIO MATCH CO.

6 BROAD ST.

"Liquor Store"

"Charleston's Leading

FINE WINES

LIQUORS AND

Imported-Domestic

LIQUOR STORE

PETER DEMOS

Phone 1353

DEMOS
RESTAURANT

BEER - WINE
TOBACCOS
PRIVATE BOOTHS

East Bay at Broad

Charleston, S. C.

CLOSE COVER BEFORE STRIKING

Matchbook advertising Demos restaurant and liquor business. *From author's collection.*

The Demos Brothers Company began advertising its "first-class restaurant and soda water fountain" at this location in 1920.[15] Harry and Peter Demos had arrived from Greece in the early 1900s and made it their mission to better the city.

The business was popular, offering hot and cold lunches throughout the day and even upgraded the space with new chairs, a lunch counter and a soda fountain in 1924. The papers noted the restaurant's success within the business district due to its fast service and good food—all of the ingredients necessary to satisfy local businessmen on their lunch breaks. The "modern" dairy lunch was even highlighted in 1924: "They have made a host of friends among the leading businessmen of the city and their well conducted place of business is headquarters for the Bay and Broad street during the social noon hour."[16]

Peter also had a successful liquor store next door and attempted to get out of the restaurant business to focus on this venture. However, the break didn't last long, and he returned after only four months. In a turn of events, the man Peter had sold the restaurant to had fallen ill and was happy to return it since he couldn't keep it open. At that point, he decided to go all in on the restaurant and bought the old Riggs building for $21,000.[17]

A testament to the frustrations of the liquor laws at that time, Peter Demos said, "I sold out my restaurant and thought I could live on my liquor business alone, but now I can't get any whiskey without going on the black market and I want to go back to my old business."[18] The restaurant was closed by the 1950s, and Peter sold the building in 1958 for $51,000.[19] Unfortunately, the original building on the corner of Broad and East Bay Streets is gone and is now home to a Wells Fargo Bank.

G & M CAFE

In much the same fashion as Harry and Peter Demos, Gerasimos "George" Magoulas also arrived in the United States by way of Greece. Leaving New York as a teenager, Magoulas set out to farm with a few friends just north of Charleston. The venture would eventually prove to be unsuccessful, but Magoulas wasn't quite ready to leave the area. After first working at a fruit stand in Charleston, he tried his hand in the restaurant industry and successfully operated G & M Cafe on Meeting Street for several years after opening in 1917.[20]

As an immigrant, Magoulas was humbled by his success, and he felt indebted to his new country and the citizens of Charleston. While he often donated to charities, his most notable move was to send extra money to the U.S. Treasury in appreciation for his citizenship. Yes, that's correct. He would make out an extra check and just hand it over to the government to use as it pleased. The amount was typically a day's receipts at the restaurant, and he felt strongly that others should follow suit. In 1941, he sent in $69 (adjusted for inflation, around $1,200 today) "in appreciation of the many privileges, rights and liberties that the United States affords."[21]

While the joy of sending extra money to the government may not have caught on, the idea for a restaurant in Magoulas's space is still going strong today. Some might remember the spot at 129 Meeting Street becoming Joseph's Restaurant in the late 1990s. The restaurant offered New Orleans–style cooking for breakfast and lunch, which Chef Joseph Passarini picked up while working in the Big Easy.

Passarini created an open kitchen to display his creation of sweet masterpieces, such as bananas foster and beignets fried to order. The business closed in 2011, when Passarini was unable to resign a lease for the building. The restaurant was eventually taken over by the Charleston Hospitality Group and is currently home to the restaurant Eli's Table.

HOTEL DINING ROOMS

While independent restaurants were growing and evolving around the city in the early twentieth century, hotel dining rooms were some of the original sources of fine dining in Charleston. Since many of these establishments seemed to be operating on the same level, a natural rivalry developed within this scene. Their growth through improvements and upgrades only served to elevate the competition and propel the dining scene forward.

THE PLANTER'S HOTEL was one of the earliest hotel establishments in the city, announcing its opening in 1803 at the corner of Meeting and Queen Streets. Even at that early time, the hotel was advertising to "entertain societies and furnish public dinners" and could accommodate up to one hundred people in the space.[22] This business eventually moved to its well-known location at 135 Church Street, which is now home to the Dock Street Theatre. It was during this time period that the Planter's Hotel earned a reputation for its food, and legend has it that the drink Planter's Punch (a dangerous mix of rum, fruit juices and grenadine) was invented here. The hotel site eventually fell into disrepair and was restored as the Dock Street Theatre in the 1930s. The historic Planter's Hotel was eventually reimagined as the Planters Inn at the corner of Meeting and North Market Street and is now home to the fine dining establishment Peninsula Grill and its world-famous coconut cake.

THE CHARLESTON HOTEL was built in 1839 at 200 Meeting Street, right across from Hyman's Seafood restaurant today. It became well known for its restaurant and bar, and a 1905 advertisement described offering "cuisine and service of the highest standard."[23] This hotel was prestigious enough to host visits from royalty as well as Presidents Taft and Roosevelt. It was also the home of the South Carolina Jockey Club, which operated the first racetrack in the United States. This meeting place, which took four years to build with its fourteen stately columns, was torn down in 1960 to make way for a more "modern" one-story hotel with 120 rooms. The papers reported that the Charleston Hotel had "lost a fight with progress," which might be the most fitting quote on record to capture the spirit of Charleston's preservation efforts.[24] In fact, the loss of the Charleston Hotel sparked quite a few debates about expanding the rules of preservation in the historic district of downtown.

THE TIMROD HOTEL AND CAFE opened in 1918 at 99 Meeting Street. It was constructed as a commercial club but was eventually converted into an inn. In an advertisement in 1919, the Timrod announced that with every cup of their coffee, customers would receive a "stimulating beverage and a nourishing food as well."[25] In the early 1900s, they offered meals like chicken with dumplings, roast pork with apple sauce, roast beef with gravy and roast veal with dressing, all ranging from fifty to sixty-five cents. A businessman's luncheon was a popular draw due to the hotel's location near the post office and the busy business district. In fact, Timrod was often referred to as the "Politician's Coffee Shop," because of the clientele.[26]

The Charleston Hotel was known for its fine dining. It played host to royals and presidents on their visits to Charleston. *From Library of Congress Prints & Photographs Division, Detroit Publishing Company Collection.*

The Timrod remained a loyal standby for coffee and food—not even a fire in March 1936 could stop its service. While the fourth floor of the hotel was destroyed by a workman's blowtorch, the subheading of the newspaper story read, "Water Damage Is Great. Dinner Served Shortly after Danger Ends."[27] At the time, Mrs. M.G. Pace ran the coffee shop and planned to serve the usual two o'clock dinner right on schedule. When the restaurant was closed for a short period of time in 1960, many patrons were worried about losing their regular hangout. It was the spot for lawyers, businessmen, government workers and pretty much anyone wishing to get their foot into the political arena. In the hustle and bustle of politics, these locals couldn't be expected to travel too far from the courthouse home base.

Luckily, the Timrod reopened after a month, and the hotel was renovated in the summer of 1960. But the writing was on the wall for the old hotel, especially with talk of plans to expand the county courthouse. J.C. Long, founder of the Beach Company, eventually purchased the Timrod Inn and surrendered his potential profits to allow the county to expand the courthouse.[28] The site was razed in 1964.

THE FORT SUMTER HOTEL opened as Charleston's first luxury hotel in January 1924, and was built on filled-in land at the foot of King Street. The ground-level floor had a dining room, which was one of the few available restaurants at the time. Among its advertised amenities was a main dining room with unique ceiling of worm-eaten pecky cypress, an expansive ballroom and the Terrace Dining Room, decorated with "soft lights radiating from three tiers of stately electric fixtures."[29]

FAMOUS
Hotel Fort Sumter

Overlooking
Charleston
Harbor

•

Dine
In Our
RAMPART
ROOM

•

FOOT OF
KING ST.

Advertisement for the Rampart Room within the Fort Sumter Hotel, 1955. *From Nelsons' Charleston City Directory, 1955.*

The Terrace Room gained popularity, and advertisements credited it as an important factor in the success of the hotel. But the decor and expansive harbor views weren't the only offerings of the Fort Sumter Hotel. Advertisements also touted its use of ice refrigeration in order to maintain the taste of food. It was a good thing that the hotel had such a luxury because, as it advertised in 1931, "Good ice refrigeration is the only way to maintain the original taste and the nutritive and palateable juices of food, for flavor is elusive and once lost cannot be regained."[30]

The restaurant would host Thanksgiving meals with stuffed grapefruit, heart of celery, roasted and stuffed South Carolina turkey and homemade fruit cake. One could venture that the baked grapefruit was quite popular, as it frequently appeared in advertisements. But don't let it fool you into thinking it was the star of the show at this location. According to a 1940 advertisement, a dinner of lobster thermidor "looks like a million, and makes you feel like a millionaire."[31]

Located on the main floor of the hotel, the Rampart Room opened in February 1954, and replaced the hotel's main dining room. The space was designed to be an informal lounge for casual dining and was decorated with a few historic touches, including a large mural of the firing on Fort Sumter. The marketing for the Rampart Room focused on the luxuries of year-round air

The Fort Sumter Hotel never quite reached its financial potential as a hotel and continues to be used as condominiums today. *From the author.*

conditioning and that famous manufactured ice—items we too easily take for granted today.

The Rampart Room frequently offered menu items such as roast beef, sirloin steak, fried chicken, Spanish mackerel, soft-shell crabs and shrimp pie. Even with air conditioning, they still focused on lighter menu items, such as jellied consommé and sugared grapes, in the summers.

The hotel had an ideal location but never saw the level of financial success it expected, which meant that it traded hands multiple times over the years. The Fort Sumter Hotel was eventually closed in 1973, when it was sold and underwent a $4 million renovation to convert the space into condominiums.[32]

Other hotels and inns also offered dining during this time period. THE BREWTON INN on Church Street opened in 1927, offering Southern comforts, such as pecan waffles, in gingham-draped dining rooms. One article described the inn's attention to detail in depth: "Guests partake of breakfast at tables set with coin silver spoons, bone—ivory handled knives and forks. Handsome antique—silver coffee urns grace each table together with sterling pepper mills and individual salt dishes."[33]

The **FRANCIS MARION HOTEL** also opened in 1924 and was the largest hotel in the city. While the hotel is still in operation today, the original Colonial Dining Room opened every spring for the tourist season and served as a banquet and convention space for the rest of the year. A 1950 advertisement told of the Charleston classics it served, such as she-crab soup, shrimp pie and hoppin' John.[34] The hotel went through a major renovation in 1955, which was when the Swamp Fox Restaurant was added. The restaurant is still in operation today.

Guests still don't have to travel far from their hotels to find fine dining in Charleston. Some of the most popular fine dining spots are located within or affiliated with a hotel. These restaurants, which include Peninsula Grill, Grill 225 and Zero Restaurant and Bar, fill up and consistently offer highly sought-after reservations.

The Francis Marion Hotel continues to operate on King Street. It is now home to the Swamp Fox Restaurant. *From the author.*

When Dining Out Was a Special Occasion

THE BEGINNINGS OF DINING OUT

Charleston's wealth of history isn't subtle. In fact, it's fairly easy to take an image from the 1800s and pinpoint a familiar landmark to anchor yourself right in the picture. While you can still touch the brick and stucco from hundreds of years ago, it takes a little more imagination to fully appreciate the important events that took place within and around these buildings.

Charleston has experienced the devastation of wars, economic booms and hardships, natural disasters and important social demonstrations. The structures provided backdrops to these moments, but the businesses within them, were the living, breathing components of that history. This meant that business owners often felt the direct impact of significant events and were forced to react and adapt in order to thrive. That's why the histories of these restaurants often offer a detailed snapshot of a way of life at a particular moment in time.

The next few decades of restaurants reflect an incredible number of significant moments in both Charleston and United States history. They remind us how different things used to be, even in a city that doesn't necessarily enjoy change. For example, in early twentieth-century Charleston, it was difficult to find *any* decent restaurant in town. In 1939, one travel writer who was visiting Charleston found themselves in a "frantic search for civilized food, winding up in a chain drugstore."[35]

King Street in the early 1900s. *From Library of Congress Prints & Photographs Division, Detroit Publishing Company Collection.*

That sentence alone is enough to appall visitors who never seem to have enough meals or enough room in their stomachs to fully appreciate everything they want to eat while in town. However, during the Great Depression, it was difficult to even convince people to go out to eat. Thus, much of the marketing content at the time was focused on keeping costs low while touting the—still persuasive—advantage of not having to wash the dishes.

Some people began to venture out of their homes for meals a bit more after World War II, especially as families began purchasing their own cars. However, the early norm in Charleston had always been to eat at home in private residences. I heard the phrase, "We just didn't go out to eat that much," over and over again in the many interviews for this book. This means that the lost restaurants of this time period often focused on offering good, hearty family meals, convenient drive-in service and very few select options of fine dining.

Robertson's Cafeteria

Edward and Julia Robertson first opened their cigar store and soda fountain at 13 Broad Street in 1914. In 1920, they extended the ground floor to create South Carolina's first cafeteria. A natural progression for their growing business, adding this type of food service was an idea they modeled after a self-service restaurant they had seen in Cleveland. Their venture was a success, especially with the neighboring businesses on Broad Street. The regular lunch crowd of lawyers, bankers and politicians were some of their best customers.

The business continued in the family when Edward and Julia's son Alex took over in 1934, after attending Rice Business College, and his brother, Thomas, joined as a partner. During the Great Depression, they survived by offering affordable specials of a meat, two vegetables, a drink and bread for only thirty-five cents.[36] It was this incredible value that Robertson's would always be known for and likely contributed to the continued growth of the business.

With the success of the original Robertson's Cafeteria, Alex and Thomas decided to open a second location at 51 Wentworth Street in 1954 and a third location west of the Ashley River in 1970 at the St. Andrew's shopping center. In 1971, the brothers decided to split the business, with Alex taking the St. Andrews location and Thomas taking over Wentworth Street.

At that time, in 1971, the brothers also made the difficult decision to close the original Broad Street Robertson's. The family had an impressive run of fifty-seven years in that location, but unfortunately, the flagship cafeteria was no longer making money. That didn't make the decision to close any easier, and as Alex told the local papers, "We ran it one year strictly out of sentiment."[37] He further explained the decision to close, stating, "The Broad Street operation—and we hate to close it because my father founded it—requires about 10 percent more payroll than the other two cafeterias. When a business begins to get to where it can't show a profit, you must disregard sentiment and do something, no matter how painful it might be."[38]

But that doesn't mean the city didn't mourn the loss of the original Robertson's Cafeteria. Jack Leland wrote about the restaurant's closing for the local paper, describing it as "a clearing house for matters political, financial, business, personal, and gossipy."[39] The closure would require folks on Broad Street to find a new location to congregate and would cause a significant disruption to the usual routine in the business district. In homage

E. H. ROBERTSON CIGAR COMPANY

C A F E T E R I A

TOBACCO and CIGARS, SODA WATER and CANDY

Quality and Premier Chocolates   Foss-Boston

PHONE 3982

13 BROAD STREET   CHARLESTON, S. C.

Robertson's Cigar Company added the state's first cafeteria in 1920. *From Walsh's Charleston City Directory, 1922.*

to the original gathering houses of Charleston's past, Leland wrote, "For Robertson's was the modern Charleston's answer to the coffee houses of yesterday."[40] It was a place to gather, to work out deals, to negotiate and disseminate. Even though the Robertson's name continued for many years to follow, the loss of the original location was memorable.

Thomas eventually retired in 1975 and closed the Wentworth Street business, leaving only the cafeteria in the St. Andrews shopping center. At that time, Alex got a little help from his son-in-law, Bruce Skidmore, who helped him run the sole surviving Robertson's.

The food at Robertson's Cafeteria was described as "traditional" Charleston, and founder Edward Robertson always emphasized fresh vegetables and high-quality meats. In fact, Edward had a farm in the north area of town that supplied poultry and eggs for the cafeteria. It was home-style Lowcountry cooking—the kind of food locals would eat in their own homes, offered at reasonable prices. The choices were seemingly endless, and everyone had a favorite.

With the three-vegetable plate, guests could fill up on rice, grits, macaroni pie, greens (spinach, turnip and collard), broccoli, brussels sprouts, squash, field peas, fried apples, okra (fried or boiled), yams and mashed potatoes. Some of the most popular items were the crab casserole, fried shrimp, deviled crab, red rice, okra gumbo, vegetable soup, Huguenot Torte and the famous Lucille's Pie, with its layers of cream cheese and chocolate pudding.

Robertson's didn't cut corners and chose to prepare most things in house as opposed to buying them premade. Of his cafeteria's offerings in 1982, Alex said, "Basically, we supply Charleston food, the kind that is distinctive of this city."[41] Many of the recipes had been accumulated by their mother over the years, though that famous Huguenot Torte recipe supposedly came home with Alex's daughter after she spent the night at a friend's house.[42]

But it wasn't just good food, it was good food at a reasonable price. Alex stated that their goal was to keep prices low so that they could be in competition with the cost of eating at home, only without having to do the dishes. This meant that when they had to raise prices, they would only do so one penny at a time. The business model was even able to compete with the fast food boom of the early 1980s. "You pay nearly as much for a hamburger as for a decent meal here," Alex said of the comparison.[43]

Robertson's didn't have to worry too much about competition. Loyal customers could be found there nearly every single day. Nothing around town offered a comparison in terms of variety and price point, and word of mouth kept the business successful. In fact, around 90 percent of the business was comprised of returning customers.[44]

That's because Robertson's wasn't just somewhere people ate once a year or for a special occasion; it was a gathering place of the community. Especially during a time of growth in Charleston, when people were venturing out to the suburbs, they could still find each other at Robertson's—whether they planned on it or not. "Charlestonians knew what was going on in Charleston because of Robertson's," one writer said in 1990.[45] This makes sense with their slogan, "Dine with us…you'll meet every friend you have."[46]

The dedication and loyalty to Robertson's could outweigh a long line out the door after a Sunday church service, and locals would often bring their out-of-town guests for proper Lowcountry cooking. Plus, with affordable prices, they could cater to retirees, Citadel cadets and even families with young children. A 1988 reviewer stated that she was thankful she didn't need to write anything critical about her visit to Robertson's. "I really wasn't worried," she explained, "I went as a child and now I go with my children."[47]

But when Hurricane Hugo hit the city in 1989, the building suffered significant damage as the roof was ripped off. It took eleven days before the roof could be replaced, and in that gap of time, the staff had to be let go. Coupling that hit with an expiring lease, Bruce Skidmore decided it was time to shut the doors for good. This was another logistical business decision with gut-wrenching consequences, as some employees had been with Robertson's for more than twenty-five years. Of the multiple news stories reporting the closure, everyone's reaction was fairly uniform: it was as if there had been a death in the family.

Several reports called the business a "victim" of Hurricane Hugo. Writer Frank Jarrell compared the closing of Robertson's to the loss of a Charleston landmark. "It was as if someone had plucked Fort Sumter out of the harbor," he wrote in 1990.[48] In a city that had lost so much to the powerful storm, the news of Robertson's closure seemed to be the last straw. In a letter to the editor on October 22, 1989, Pauline Sottile wrote:

I could handle Hugo's blows—leaking roofs, flooded basement, smashed-in car door, broken windows, mud and water in my beach house—but, when I read in the paper that Robertson's cafeteria was closing its doors forever because of Hugo, I cried! I am sure the owners are doing what they feel is right, but I'm sure they have no idea how many people in the Charleston area are as upset as I! Please reconsider![49]

Just one day before the equipment was to be sold at auction, William L. Merrell, who owned Po Folks Restaurant in nearby Mount Pleasant, negotiated the lease. Because the family didn't sell the rights to the name, Merrell decided to rename the restaurant the "Cafeteria at St. Andrew's Shopping Center," with the understanding that people would likely continue to refer to it as "Robertson's" no matter what they named it. They were also able to hire some longtime employees, and with them came the regular crowds. Charlestonians were like "kids at Christmastime. You can see the glimmer in their eyes. People say they're so glad we're back," said employee Randy Coats.[50]

Merrell, the new owner, added, "I can tell you that from my experience, this cafeteria was like a cult."[51] Even during the restaurant's post-storm renovation, locals would stop by and call, frequently checking for updates on the future reopening. In one interview, a few locals said they hadn't even had a vegetable since the hurricane "and some had to learn how to cook after the cafeteria closed. The hurricane took away some old habits," Coats explained.[52]

Alas, it's not always easy to re-create lightning in a bottle, and the cafeteria, which eventually changed to the name Fyshbyrne's, closed for good in 1992. Representatives stated they were doing about "half the business we were doing five years ago" by the time they closed.[53] While the regular crowd continued to show up, it appeared that the cafeteria suffered when others didn't know they were there. A large sign that said "Cafeteria" came down in the hurricane, and the new owners weren't allowed to replace it. "People didn't know we were open after Hugo," manager Frank DuRoss said.[54] One might assume the loss of the cafeteria for a second time would ease the blow just a bit, but this was not so for regular patron George C. Evans, who, upon learning the news, said, "You must be teasing! I might just jump out my window."[55]

Harold's Cabin

Harold's Cabin began as a snowball stand run by an ambitious teenager in 1928. At that time, a building resembling a log cabin stood at the intersection of President and Congress Streets. The structure was lit with kerosene lamps and sat in front of an unpaved street. Harold Jacobs operated the business, although he did require his mother's help so that he could also attend the High School of Charleston. The Sno-Balls—shaved ice covered with sweet syrup—were sold for either three or five cents, depending on the size, and came in flavors of strawberry, grape, chocolate and orange.

The landlord expanded the building the following year, and the family was able to establish a small corner grocery store while they lived up above. As the venture proved successful, the building was expanded once again in 1950 and added a delicatessen. Harold's father also began his search for unique and hard-to-find food items. While the clientele for such items was limited at the time, these were the rare products for which Harold's Cabin would eventually be known.

As the business grew, the need for more space became apparent. So, in September 1953, Harold's Cabin made the move to an impressive building on Wentworth Street, just west of King Street. The business' success from such humble beginnings was described by the local paper as, "from log cabin to emporium."[56]

There was a balcony along the back of the store with two staircases on either side, all framed by a "lavender tinted wrought-iron rail."[57] The main floor also featured a waterfall that spouted right out of the west wall. The community was overwhelmed by the multitude of choices available within the shop, specifically the sheer number of different imported cheeses.

An advertisement at the time described the many features of the store, including a wine cellar, sandwich balcony, delivery service and gift wrapping. Harold's Cabin offered thousands of products that couldn't be found anywhere else. Dubbed "Charleston's most fascinating food store," it had snails, fried caterpillars, grasshoppers and chocolate-covered ants. It became so popular that tourist buses would make stops at the store. This location offered the city's first frozen foods—a feat that required a little faith from the bank when Harold went to borrow money for refrigeration equipment. The inspiration came after a friend showed him a frozen food package from New York. The $500 loan was initially turned down, as the idea of frozen food seemed ridiculous. It was filled later by another banker who was a bit more interested in Harold's revolutionary idea.[58]

While this spot may seem more like a grocery or specialty food shop, Harold's Cabin also had the "Sandwich Balcony," which became a regular lunch spot for many locals in the '50s and '60s. When they decided to try opening for Sunday lunch, they offered a choice between a cold buffet or a hot meal prepared by the staff. Even after extensive advertisement, they only sold a few of the hot meals. What followed was an advertising gimmick of pure genius by Harold Jacobs: renaming the chicken dish "Charleston Baked Chicken Magnolia," with an "Old Jacobs family recipe" nostalgia to finish off the description.[59]

While the advertisement was a bit of a stretch, it absolutely worked wonders. Charleston Baked Chicken Magnolia became incredibly popular at Harold's Cabin and was even served at catering events. Harold shared the recipe with the local paper in 1996. It was composed of chicken in a brown sauce made with a clear broth, Kitchen Bouquet, Lawry's seasoned salt, chopped parsley and celery. A magnolia leaf that the family would purchase from the vendors outside of the post office would add the necessary Charleston flair to complete the dish.

Harold and his wife, Lillian, successfully ran Harold's Cabin for years, until they decided to sell the business. In October 1964, an open letter from F. Marion Brabham, owner of the Meeting Street Piggly Wiggly, ran in the paper. In a testament to how little Charlestonians enjoy change, he acknowledged that "progress is inevitable, however, often this same progress, which affords us such a wonderful way of life, today, kills the traditions and institutions that we all hold dear to our hearts. One traditional landmark in Charleston, Harold's Cabin, long regarded as a gourmets' paradise, fell victim to this progress."[60]

Brabham went on to state that he was able to purchase the business and would run it at its Wentworth location for a period of time. However, Harold's Cabin would eventually be absorbed into the Meeting Street Piggly Wiggly as a separate department under the supervision of Mr. and Mrs. Jacobs.

Harold remained on staff as the manager and set up the catering and delicatessen services in the Piggly Wiggly. He also worked hard to train staff members who carried on after his retirement. At least the move to the Piggly Wiggly should have cleared up the confusion that Harold's Cabin didn't offer rooms to rent, a common issue during the time of the Jacobses' business.

Even after retirement in 1983, Harold continued to work, promoting group tourism with the Adventure Travel Agency and maintaining a pivotal role in Charleston's Jewish community. He passed away at the age of ninety-

Harold's Cabin has been reimagined at its original location on the corner of President and Congress Streets. *From the author.*

six in 2009, but his legacy was not forgotten. In 2016, Harold's Cabin was brought back to life at its original location on the corner of President and Congress Streets. This was led by the team at Yarrum Properties, which happens to include Charleston's favorite celebrity, Bill Murray, and co-owner John Schumacher.

Schumacher was motivated to be a part of this project after learning the story of Harold's Cabin. In an email interview with the author, he stated, "It was the soul of the entire story of Harold, Lillian and his parents. A 15-year-old boy selling Sno-Balls on the corner of President and Congress Streets and then convincing his parents to open the mercantile before there was electricity in the neighborhood." Schumacher said he felt a sense of obligation to share the story with others.

In the reimagined restaurant, people often comment on what they remember from the original Harold's Cabin, such as house-made pickles, Sno-Balls, the variety of cheeses and the fact that Harold's Cabin was the first store in Charleston to offer Ritz Crackers. In keeping with these memories, Schumacher said that "the house-made Savoure cheese spread was the item that most folks were (and still are) passionate about. We offer the spread in our retail section and occasionally include it on menu specials."

The community is incredibly fortunate that stories such as these can continue to live on through the work of people like Schumacher, who summed up his experience in this restaurant project:

> *There are three generations of Charlestonians who have memories of Harold's Cabin. The youngest remember when there was a [Harold's Cabin] corner deli section in the Piggly Wiggly, a fewer number remember the second, a two-story retail and restaurant [Harold's Cabin] location on Wentworth Street (the building is no longer there), but on very rare occasions we see folks (usually in their 80s or older) who make it to us who remember coming to the original Harold's Cabin. When they walk in you can see their eyes light up and they have the look of a nine-year-old kid reliving a memory. Those moments are both humbling and a true honor to be a part of.*

LaBrasca's Spaghetti House and Pizzeria

LaBrasca's wasn't the only spaghetti house around Charleston in the mid-1900s, but it certainly stood out among the crowd. In fact, nearly every restaurant owner I spoke with recalled dining here with their own families. The memories that remain from this special place may have something to do with the people who ran it and the warm, inviting environment they managed to create in their restaurant space.

The restaurant was opened in 1943 by Effie and George LaBrasca with a $10,000 loan from a friend.[61] George was from Sicily and Effie was born in Newfoundland, Canada, but together they would create a local empire of American-Italian-Chinese food. Effie had been cooking for years and figured that she might just be able to make a bit of money off her talent. Possessing a unique culinary instinct, she was the kind of cook who could make adjustments by taste, not by the strict rules of the recipe.

LaBrasca's originally offered Italian food, but when George Mark joined the restaurant as the cook, the menu adapted and evolved. Mark was born in China and was able to bring his culinary talent to the restaurant shortly after it opened. Since Mr. LaBrasca was also named George, Mark earned the nickname Uncle George. The name was appropriate, considering Mark was like an honorary member of the LaBrasca family and a fixture in the restaurant for decades.

Perhaps this variety in the menu helped the LaBrasca family make a name for themselves in the restaurant community, even during a time when people weren't eating out much. After all, pizza, spaghetti and chicken chop suey had the ability to please a varied crowd. But LaBrasca's wasn't just a place to eat—it became an important local meeting place. The archives listed page after page of events meeting up at LaBrasca's. People would gather after a dance, baseball game or junior club meeting. Citadel cadets would often come by for Sunday supper as a chance to skip out on the less-than-favorable cafeteria food.

The group eventually added LaBrasca Pizzeria next door, and the Spaghetti House was rebuilt in 1967 to add two separate kitchens—one for Italian food and another for Chinese food—as well as additional seating and a waterfall feature. In their success, Effie, affectionately known as Mama, still took every opportunity to make sure people were well fed and well taken care of. While she was talented in the kitchen, she didn't isolate herself in the back of the restaurant. People could find her working the crowds and getting to know everyone from any walk of life. In 1987, a local writer stated that "LaBrasca's was one of those places where anybody could feel at home, mostly because of Mama's presence."[62]

Her kindness was felt across the community, as she was constantly looking for ways to help those in need. Sometimes that meant feeding people at her restaurant even if they couldn't pay or seeking out others in the community to help pay their rent, utilities or medical bills.

George LaBrasca passed away in 1969, and Effie and her daughter, Rose, ran the restaurant together for a while afterward. But the rigors of maintaining two restaurants downtown eventually became more of a challenge than they were up for, not to mention the fact that Effie's son had opened a LaBrasca East in Mount Pleasant in 1974. So, in the summer of 1975, Effie and Rose packed up the original LaBrasca's. While downtown would forever be the heart of their business, Effie continued to place family above anything else.

"It broke my heart to let the places go after having them for 33 years. It just gave me a horrible feeling," Effie said in an interview in 1975.[63] Her son needed her help, but unfortunately, by that time it was a bit too late for his restaurant, and it closed a few months later. They went bankrupt in the process, and Effie reported that the family "lost hundreds of thousands of dollars."[64] Effie continued to be ever humble and ever grateful in her life and didn't let anything slow her down, even into her seventies.

After a yearlong break, Effie and Rose opened Mama's Tea Room on Sullivan's Island, serving Italian food once again. When Effie passed away in 1987, at the age of ninety-eight, the entire community felt the loss of such a passionate and caring restaurateur. Mama's Tea Room closed the following year with a simple thank you from the family posted in the local papers.

While the lot on the corner of King and Cleveland Streets is now empty, the fond memories of LaBrasca's are abundant. Janson L. Cox's letter to the editor shortly after Effie's passing perfectly summed up her legacy with the statement, "To so many people, her restaurant was a haven of good eating and family love."[65]

PROHIBITION IN THE SOUTH

The South felt the effects of Prohibition well before and well after federal restrictions, which really just meant we had a few more years to figure out how to work the system. Even in 1893, South Carolina had laws limiting the sale of liquor to government-run dispensaries. The restrictive law meant that many honest restaurants, saloons, and grocery stores in Charleston became home to "blind tigers," what we called speakeasies in the South. There were certainly tales of raids around the city, but law enforcement didn't make it too difficult for business owners to continue their suddenly illegal operations.

Some restaurant owners weren't even shy about the potential consequences of their offerings, with a bold few even advertising the availability of alcohol right in the local papers. Take King's Restaurant at 337 King Street, which was opened in 1919 by George D. Phillips, a hotel operator from New York City. Phillips quickly found success in Charleston's restaurant business and had done so well by 1922 that he was able to upgrade the restaurant with modern amenities and promises of fast, high-quality service and food.[66]

The menu promoted not only seafood and steaks but also illegal alcohol. King's Restaurant was even advertising a free lunch with the purchase of "a schooner of good old draught beer" in May 1933, months before the official repeal of Prohibition.[67] This advertisement was evidence of either shameless disregard for the law or the lack of any concrete repercussions at the time.

While Prohibition was lifted in 1933, each state was left to determine their own liquor laws. South Carolina didn't allow the retail sale of liquor until two whole years later. Even with the lessened restrictions, restaurants still weren't allowed to sell liquor drinks to patrons. This regulation continued to put a damper on the bottom line for many establishments and forced some owners to find other ways around the law.

Some restaurants attempted a runaround by claiming that they were placing a patron's personal liquor on "deposit," thus allowing them to order by the drink until it was emptied.[68] Others simply sold drink mixers with ice to be combined with liquor the guests would bring in. Since these bottles usually came straight from the liquor store, the practice was affectionately known as "brown bagging."

These restrictive liquor laws were in place for nearly forty years in Charleston, until the "mini-bottle" law was passed in 1973. This allowed restaurants to serve liquor drinks of less than two ounces, and bar shelves were quickly filled with those tiny airplane bottles. Many local restaurateurs had played a significant role in getting the law passed, traveling to Columbia and speaking out about the need for change.

While most other states eventually moved on from similar laws, South Carolina kept the "mini-bottle" law in place for thirty-three long years. The very last state to repeal such a law, it's almost shocking to realize bartenders didn't start free-pouring drinks in Charleston until 2006. The newfound freedom required a bit of an adjustment, as bars had to reconfigure their storage to account for larger bottles. But more importantly, bartenders had the opportunity to get creative with a much wider variety of alcohol. As if we were making up for lost time, many people credit this freedom with bringing a lively cocktail scene to Charleston and certainly changing the landscape of bars and restaurants downtown.[69]

Henry's

Yes, Henry's still exists on North Market Street, but that's not technically the restaurant we are discussing. We're talking about the old Henry's. When people reminisce about the original version of Henry's that began in 1932, the first thing they mention is how fancy it used to be—the epitome of fine dining at the time. All of my experiences at Henry's have been in shorts and flip-flops, so I couldn't quite relate to this version until diving into the research. I was pleasantly enlightened by the prestige and elegance of what once was.

The story begins with Henry Otto Hasselmeyer, a first-generation German immigrant who began a grocery store and saloon at 54 Market Street in 1892. When the restrictions on liquor sales came into effect, he, like many others, just sort of kept his saloon business going. Since this landed him on the wrong side of the law, Hasselmeyer's establishment was frequently the subject of raids by law enforcement.

Two of these instances in 1897 were particularly notable due to Hasselmeyer's quick thinking. While his partner stalled police downstairs, Henry allegedly got to work getting rid of the alcoholic evidence. The report from March 1897 states, "It was not raining, but there was a rainy day rattle in the gutter pipes."[70] One of the officers claimed it was beer flowing down those gutters, but Hasselmeyer's efficiency left no trace of evidence by the time the officers made their way upstairs.

In another instance a few months later, Henry's wife joined in on the shenanigans. It was said that "the searchers after booze allege that Mrs. Hasselmeyer concealed a keg of beer under her clothes at the time the raid was made."[71] While she remained steadfast in her refusal to move during the raid in what is now the Whiskey Room, arrests were made on both occasions for the Hasselmeyers' interference with the investigations.

The illicit liquor trade was lucrative for Henry, but he eventually found even greater success when he turned his grocery store into a restaurant in 1932. While it might seem like prime real estate today, opening a business in the market area was a gamble. The area was often described as "seedy," and the original City Market was still in operation. At that time, visitors wouldn't find local crafts or artisan soaps for sale but rather raw scraps of meat tossed into the streets and a few buzzards (or as we lovingly called them, "Charleston Eagles") hovering for their next meal from the butchers.

In this perhaps unlikely spot, Hasselmeyer jumped all in and eventually earned a reputation for serving high-quality food with impeccable service. Originally intended to be called "Henry Hasselmeyer's," the restaurant officially opened in 1932 as the simplified "Henry's" because the sign painter charged by the letter.[72] From these days, many people recall the black and white tiled floor, round golden oak tables in the dining rooms and a nautical-themed bar area. The Hunt Room and the Collegiate Room could be found upstairs, along with a few games of poker. The waiters wore crisp white jackets, and the service was distinctly elegant. Keeping the restaurant legacy in the family, Henry Hasselmeyer Jr. eventually took over the business, and many people fondly remember his sister, Marguerite, as the hostess—a Henry's staple since 1941.

To fully appreciate Henry's offerings, I had the opportunity to flip through some original 1940s menus that reside in the South Carolina Historical Society Archives. They were elegant in their simplicity, and the typed menu

Market Street's infamous buzzards ruled the area in their quest for meat scraps. *From Library of Congress Prints & Photographs Division, Detroit Publishing Company Collection.*

changed daily. Another example of my preconceived notions getting in the way, I was even taken aback by the formality of the spelling out of the date: "Tuesday September 4th, 1945."

On this particular day, the lunch entrées ranged from $0.85 to $1.25 and included items such as "sautéed fresh calf's liver with pork sausage and bacon" and "Henry's special green shrimp à la creole with rice timbale." Vegetables included steamed whole rice, boiled potatoes, string beans, garden beets, creamed carrots and stewed eggplant. The idea of fruited Jell-O as a dessert option was a little jarring, but they also offered cantaloupe, apple cobbler and ice cream as a last course.

The dinner menu was even more upgraded and entitled "Henry's Selective Table D'Hôte Dinner Menu." The entrées were more expensive, ranging from $1.25 to $1.75, and included options such as "poached filet of Charleston snapper with Wando sauce" or "sautéed fresh select sweet breads à la American with pimento sauce."[73]

Henry's menu from the 1940s. *From Leo Chiagkouris.*

Despite these many offerings, Henry's ultimately became known for its seafood. In fact, a 1949 article pointed out the lack of local restaurants specializing in seafood—a moment in Charleston's restaurant history that's still a little difficult to comprehend. In this market, Henry's had the opportunity to stand out, reporting the majority of its sales—75 percent— from seafood, with a clientele of mostly locals.[74]

While he never received much press, Henry Jr. referred to the longtime cook, John Bolton, as "the best cook in Charleston."[75] Like many Henry's employees who stayed on for decades, John started there when he was just seventeen years old, only leaving for a few years during his overseas service in France during World War II.

Perhaps with a hint of that European flair, the Henry's menu was filled with an extensive range of "à la." Simply flipping through a week's worth of menus from 1945, I found at least eighteen iterations of "à la." Dishes were served à la American, à la Colbert, à la Thermidor, à la Key West, à la Milanaise, à la Poulette, à la Newburg, à la Gomez and many, many more.[76] Some of these dishes were named for local spots like the Wando River, while others were named for chefs and notable patrons. Regardless, it was an impressive and ever-changing menu.

Pompano à la Gherardi was one of Henry's most popular dishes and was even featured on a promotional postcard for the restaurant. The pompano was stuffed with crab and shrimp and then topped with onions, sherry, bacon and olives. The she-crab soup was another incredibly popular dish, but Henry's classic method of preparation needed to be explained to those diners who thought their soup tasted a bit off. "If you think your She-Crab Soup has a taste you don't recognize, it's because we put sherry in it," the signs on the table clarified.[77] Regardless of what people chose to eat, every meal started with a complimentary relish tray of celery, radish, pickles and a cheese spread with just a bit of kick, perhaps from the horseradish or hot sauce it contained.[78]

The bar at Henry's became one of the city's first hoppin' spots for happy hour and quick lunch service. A cozy spot with a ship's wheel hung on the wall above the old cash register, flanked by images of ships on either side and a bell hanging directly above the register. There were boxes of cigars and packs of smokes for sale behind the bar and chilled wines nestled in the wall. While locals got to know Henry's as their spot, it was also becoming known around the country. *McCall's* named it one of the best 144 restaurants in the United States in 1955, with a special feature and recipe in the magazine, while it was given the Duncan Hines Institute award for excellence in 1959.

Henry's Restaurant circa 1963. *From Historic Charleston Foundation Archives.*

Time magazine called it one of the top ten United States restaurants, while *Venture* magazine distinguished it as its Critic's Choice.

Henry's growing reputation even brought in a big-name crowd that included Bing Crosby, Bob Hope, Frank Murphy, Joan Crawford and Nelson Eddie, just to name a few.

The family-owned tradition at Henry's lived on for years, as Henry Jr. would check in nearly every morning and Marguerite happened to live right next door. At that point, however, Henry Jr. had passed the baton to his son-in-law George Brownell. When Marguerite passed in the 1980s, she was one of the last official Hasselmeyer names connected to the restaurant.

While Henry's was known for its prestige, elegance and fine dining beginnings, by the end of the 1970s it had lost a bit of its luster. An article in the *International Review of Food and Wine* magazine from April 1979, was a harsh indication of how the business had changed. When writer Miriam Ungerer returned to Charleston, where she had spent time as a child, she wrote of Henry's, "Where were the white tablecloths, gleaming silver, crystal, dignified old waiters in white coats? Where, indeed, was *anything* I thought I had remembered?"[79] Even when local food critic Frank Jarrell revisited the restaurant in 1981, he noted that the service was up to par, as was expected with the Henry's name, but the food had left him wanting.[80]

To be fair, managing such a large piece of real estate with an even bigger reputation couldn't have been easy, which is likely why Brownell eventually put the buildings up for sale. The property sat on the market for a while, looking a bit like a money pit to potential investors. It was a large, historic set of five buildings that hadn't had a face-lift since the 1930s. The property had seen hurricanes and tornadoes and was in desperate need of a makeover.

Leo Chiagkouris was a young, local restaurateur who owned Swensen's Ice Cream Factory and Restaurant in the market area. In fact, he used to park his car in the dirt lot behind Henry's and had a feeling he could do something with the property. When he purchased Henry's for $1 million in 1985, he was mostly interested in the property. Little did he know he would fall in love with the business. While he vowed to maintain the traditions of Henry's, locals knew the sale of the restaurant was the end of an era. Many came out that last day in August, in the pouring-down rain, to say their goodbyes. Some traditions of the original Henry's menu are continued on by Hank's Seafood Restaurant on nearby Hayne Street, as it still serves the classic Seafood à la Wando, and many say the waiters' white jackets and black ties are an homage to the classic restaurant.

Chiagkouris was very young when he purchased Henry's in 1985, which might have been a good thing, considering the amount of work he needed to pour into his new investment. In talking about his journey of owning Henry's, Chiagkouris reiterated the power of southern hospitality and kindness. As someone who clearly loves this city, he is quick to invite everyone to experience his restaurant as a community meeting place as he continues to honor the history of the Hasselmeyer family.

Even as one of the most famous restaurants in the city, Henry's place on Market Street hasn't been without its own unique challenges. A recession, followed by a reduction in street parking on Market Street, had an impact on the area. Chiagkouris even has a few choice words for those green poles the city put in to block parking spaces. By his observations, the renovation left Market Street looking empty and dead—a bit too quiet to attract customers. For a long time, Market Street just wasn't what it used to be. "It's like someone you love, maintain her, don't change her," Chiagkouris said of all the changes during an interview with the author. His recommendation would be to add back more parking and green trees—the sort of things that have allowed other streets in the city to flourish.

Regardless of the many transformations of Market Street, the recent international press and attention on the city has helped bring business back to the area. Chiagkouris said it took eight years to get business back to what

Henry's underwent significant renovations after being sold in 1985. *From Leo Chiagkouris.*

it was, and Henry's had its biggest year ever in 2018. The restaurateur has never been more appreciative of what he owns and even got a bit choked up while on the subject. When explaining this gratitude, he said, "My customers and staff make me so happy, it blows my mind."

Once called "the grand old gentleman of the Charleston restaurant scene,"[81] Henry's has taken different forms over the years, and while the original may be considered lost, the legacy continues on in its own way.

CURB SERVICE

When scanning through decades of classified ads, you're bound to find a few gems that jump out of the monotonous text. Some were a little obnoxious in their specificity, like the advertisement to fill a hostess position on the Scarlett O'Hara that required "an attractive face and figure, long dark hair, sparkling personality, good memory for names and faces."[82] However, the more vague positions struck even more interest, like the "salad girl" mentioned in that same advertisement or the even more confusing "curb girl" requests in the 1940s. Forgive my ignorance on this one, but it sure took a moment to process what in the world they were looking for. It started to make a bit more sense when placed in the context of the changing times of the 1940s.

At this point, people were buying cars and traveling farther distances. Who wanted to walk when they could cruise around? And who wanted to get out of that fancy new car when they could have service right to the curb? (See, now it all makes sense.) With an increase in leisure time, people found new meeting places in drive-in restaurants. And while the heyday of drive-ins was the '50s and '60s, they would eventually be replaced by the desire to sit in a more climate-controlled environment. Sadly, in Charleston, many of these restaurants—especially around the area of Spring and Cannon Streets—were eventually replaced by fast-food chain restaurants.

The Fork

When the Fork opened in 1945, it didn't really have to advertise a specific address but instead a localized area between Spring and Cannon Streets, near the Ashley River Bridge. A reminder of how things change, this was at a time when there wasn't much out there on the "outskirts" of town.

The menu offerings were perfect for a filling meal consisting of steaks, barbecue and fried chicken. There was curb service for taking lunch to-go on the way in or out of the peninsula. The business did well, eventually opening another location in Mount Pleasant, as well as a sandwich shop downtown.

Renovations in 1951 expanded the restaurant with a $50,000 investment, adding modern amenities, a dining room finished in knotty pine, a private dining room area and full air conditioning. The grounds around the building were even raised two and a half feet for the ever-appreciated "high and dry" parking area downtown.[83]

The building sustained a serious fire in 1972 and sadly sat for quite some time as both an eyesore and a reminder of days past. After a brief delay to its demolition while the city searched for the property owners, the location was razed in 1973 to make way for a Hardee's.

Kate's Drive-In Restaurant

Next to Bootle's in West Ashley, Kate Lubelsky had the second drive-in in the Charleston area, but the first on the peninsula. Lubelsky would become a powerhouse in the Charleston restaurant scene but opened her first restaurant on Upper King Street in 1936. The place was called Kate's Tearoom and began with a $150 loan.[84] The restaurant was a family-run business, with Kate's husband and eventually six of her children helping out. They did a lot of business during that time, even in the Depression era. Her success was likely the result of using quality ingredients and never skimping on the portion sizes. Kate's Tearoom sold three hundred or more sizzling steaks—a dish Kate's son Joe claimed to have brought to Charleston—a day.[85]

The business did well with eat-in and take-out orders, and Kate expanded and moved into a lot on the corner of King and Spring Streets. When Kate's Drive-In Restaurant opened in 1946, it offered an impressive 129 different kinds of sandwiches. Kate also created her own recipe for onion rings after trying them in Atlanta, and in a 1980 interview, she explained how they became a staple of her restaurant: "At first my customers dunked them in the coffee thinking they were doughnuts. But they figured it out and they really liked them. Why, those onion rings were the talk of the town."[86]

She eventually moved the business to North Charleston in 1961 and changed the name to Mama Kate's to avoid confusing it with her other establishments in the area. While it was a popular spot in its new home, Mama Kate's was eventually lost to the development of the Mark Clark Expressway.

Piggy Park Drive-In

Cars would file in under the awning of the Piggy Park. They were filled with teenagers cruising for a hangout or families grabbing a quick bite. Joe Bessinger's spot was the beginning of the famous barbecue family's empire of eateries. The family would grow to add more Piggy Parks around town, but they also branched off into the more familiar Bessinger or Melvin's Barbeque names, including that signature mustard-based barbeque sauce.

Like other drive-ins at the time, locals could snag a cherry Coke, a milkshake, fries or a banana split, with curb service right to their car doors. Piggy Park was the place for anyone to be, considering downtown Charleston closed up shop fairly early in those days. Along with the change in the times, it became less logical to continue operating curb service, as many businesses were switching to dine-in service. The last of the Piggy Park Drive-Ins closed in the mid-1980s.

The Patio Drive-In

Opened in 1954, the Patio Drive-In was everything a teenager would want in the '50s. They could find the perfect spot for their personalized rides, order curb service of barbecue, greasy onion rings, hamburgers and soft drinks, while hanging with their friends on a Saturday night. Perhaps the most memorable part of the Patio was the local DJ who perched in his glass booth on top of the restaurant. People could attach a song request or a friendly shout-out request via the fishing pole with a clothespin attached to it. After a date night, or a few hours at Skateland, the Patio was the place to be. Suffering a similar fate as other restaurants in the area, the Patio was eventually torn down in 1978 to make way for a fast-food restaurant.

LOCAL CLASSICS

As dining out became more of a regular occurrence, Charlestonians began to develop their go-to spots for daily meals served with a healthy dose of local gossip. These restaurants offered a place of comfort and familiarity that all but eliminated the extensive debate over where to grab a meal.

Pete's Restaurant

In 1947, Pete Lempesis advertised his restaurant's new, modernized space on Upper King Street. He made sure to remind people that it was the "same old Pete" that had been operating since 1940, including fountain service and fast, yet courteous, service.[87]

When Lempesis died in 1958, the business was run by his wife, Catherine "Kitty" Lempesis, for another two years. Even though she ended up selling the restaurant, she kept it in the family, with Pete's brother Gus taking the reins in 1960. At that point, the business wasn't doing quite as well as it once had. That meant when Gus took over, he'd start his day seated at the bar with a newspaper, unsure of when he'd see his first customer. But once the community got to know Gus, the business started blossoming again.

This was also a time when the Charleston Revitalization Office was working to get business back to Upper King Street. Pete's was considered a mom-and-pop place that added value and character to the neighborhood. Gus described his typical clientele as other business owners, police officers and political figures. The regulars ordered off a menu that offered a few classics, such as hamburgers, cheeseburgers and three different types of Greek chicken.

When Gus eventually left the business in 1986, one customer said, "Gus is a legend, a fixture on this street. We hate to see him go."[88] Michael and Bonnie Brateman were then in charge, assuming the heavy weight of managing a beloved institution. They were careful not to make too many changes in their ownership, especially since the business had been virtually the same since the 1940s. But that didn't stop people from pointing out the differences and offering advice like, "That's not the way Gus used to do it."[89]

The crowds still came in for a quick meal and expected fast service. The Brateman's realized that their restaurant was the kind of place that attracted a regular local scene with conversations that often drifted outside of a single table. It was a one-stop shop for the city's best gossip. Unfortunately, they only owned the restaurant for three years before Hurricane Hugo struck and devastated the building on King Street. The Bratemans waited months for the news of the loan required to rebuild the business, as they needed around $50,000 to restore the building.[90]

The area around Upper King had been slated for revitalization prior to the storm and efforts ramped right back up afterward. However, business owners were in a bit of a quandary at the time. Some were hoping to sell their buildings for a high price after the storm, while others looked to retire. Many were just waiting for the Visitor's Center to open in their area with the expectation that tourists and foot traffic would follow. It was a time of gambling on an unknown future, and in this uncertainty, Pete's never reopened.

People in the neighborhood were saddened by the loss of Pete's. It was the kind of place where people could eat regularly because the food was reasonably priced, and the family-run nature was an added bonus. While the owners had remained hopeful about going back into business, the high restoration price tag likely led to the decision to make a change.

The Goodie House

Some restaurants are remembered not just for the food but also for the experience they offered. The Goodie House happens to be one of those places. The small diner began in 1948, when R.C. and Ruth Parke opened the restaurant at 168 Calhoun Street. The Williams family purchased the business in 1970 and Mr. Bill Williams's sons, C.M. and Cliff, eventually took over the reins. Cliff ran the food and C.M. dealt with the customers— roles they both fit into well.

The setting was quaint—a tiny house filled by one counter spanning the width of the building and barely enough room for twelve stools. They were the kind of seating options that were just uncomfortable enough to keep the crowd moving, which was a helpful tactic when people waited up to an hour just to grab a spot, or when the lines reached out the door during a lunch rush. There was nothing pretentious about the Goodie House. The walls were green, the countertop was a humble laminate and the appliances were still chugging from the 1950s.

The patrons were college students, professors, kids going to Bishop England and blue- and white-collar workers, all sitting side by side at the same counter. When the restaurant was open for twenty-four hours a day, seven days a week, the late-night crowd could stumble in for that perfectly filling mix of hash browns and cheeseburgers in the hopes of thwarting a hangover.

The Goodie House was good in many ways. The menu even stated, "We only serve the best—the best food to the best people."[91] Its food was a source of comfort, especially for the many College of Charleston students and Citadel cadets who would find their way in on a daily basis. Greasy—but in the most delicious way—chili, grits, pecan waffles, eggs, bacon, ham, sausage and buttery toast or biscuits were all perfect options. The hash browns were sprinkled with just a touch of paprika for a little something special, while the pies were "legendary," likely due to their homemade crust and real whipped cream. Flavors like banana cream, chocolate cream, coconut and pecan usually warranted a waitlist during the holiday season.

The fact that C.M. and Cliff knew their customer's names, and possibly even their whole families, made the place special. Even better, they might have known exactly what customers wanted before they even ordered. When the College of Charleston grew, the Goodie House became known as the place to grab a hearty breakfast in preparation for a big test or a haven to lament over the rough results. Many students even ran a tab at the Goodie House, which was a more comforting choice than a college meal plan.

When the building suffered a significant fire, started by an electrical short, in December 1992, the Williamses had to close the restaurant for six to eight weeks. Even the temporary closure sent people into a frenzy. Kaki Mahoney, a college student, stated, "It was always a comfort to know it was there. Charleston has changed too much and this was a part of Charleston that hadn't changed."[92]

Perhaps that's the most comforting feeling a restaurant can offer. A place where customers feel seen, where crusts are cut off of a sandwich before someone even needs to specify. A place that seems a lot like a home away from home. A place where things stay the same—predictable and easy.

So, when the end really came in 1996, people had a difficult time accepting the decision. There were ransom note–style letters threatening retaliation, with intimidating messages like, "If you close the Goodie House, I will have to kill both of you—And your pie cook too!!!"[93] Luckily these pranks didn't stress the owners too much, and they took it all as a testament to the loyalty they had built over the years.

People swiped old menus and grabbed their branded T-shirts, and a local restaurateur even scooped up the famous Goodie House stools. Loyal customers brought in their children to get a taste before a piece of their history was gone forever. In the ultimate swing from small, family business to a large corporation, the Goodie House became a Starbucks to fulfill the caffeine needs of the college campus. Now an even further cry from the greasy diner it used to be, the building is home to a Clean Juice, although many say that might be just as well, because nothing could truly replace the Goodie House.

Everett's Restaurant

Everett Presson didn't necessarily know how to run a restaurant when he arrived in Charleston and purchased Beshere's Grill in the 1940s. In fact, he had grown up very poor, living in a tenement home as a sharecropper with a fifth-grade education. But what he lacked in insider knowledge, he more than made up for with a strong work ethic and a respect for his community that would eventually lead him to great success.

Shortly after acquiring his new restaurant, Presson was unexpectedly drafted into the war and signed up for the Coast Guard. As a restaurant owner, he was assigned to be a ship's cook, though he had absolutely no experience cooking. Fortunately, he would eventually be allowed to stay in Charleston with his restaurant under the strict conditions that he would remain in uniform and not work.

This unusual situation led Presson's wife, Dolly, to work diligently in the kitchen to keep the business running while he made sure his Coast Guard buddies had a great time. He succeeded in his hospitality, and these men frequently came to eat at his restaurant. The Pressons' hard work didn't go unrewarded, and they counted out more money piled up on the mattress at home than they had ever imagined.

In that restaurant on King Street, which would eventually be renamed "Everett's Restaurant," William Deas came to work after his time working for Mayor Rhett. Described as a "stately, refined gentleman," Deas had quite the presence in the kitchen. When Presson purchased the restaurant, Deas made his special crab soup as a welcome and was eventually promoted to head chef.

The crab soup had its own origin story and a legacy that lives on to this day. William Deas had worked as a butler and cook for Mayor R. Goodwyn Rhett at 116 Broad Street, a building now known as the John Rutledge House Inn. When Deas was tasked with enhancing a "pale" soup for a formal dinner, he found that orange crab legs did the trick to enhance both the color and the flavor. But it was the crab roe, or egg mass, that made all the difference, even though the vendors at the time charged an extra ten cents a dozen for this luxury. Legend has it that this was the soup created and served to President Taft upon his visit to Charleston in 1909. The original recipe printed in the newspaper in 1958 was so focused on our fresh Lowcountry ingredients that it even began with the suggestion of getting your crab net.[94]

Everett's son, also named Everett Presson, still holds the handwritten recipe by Deas. Yes, there is a secret ingredient missing in the recipe that's been

The John Rutledge House is supposedly the birthplace of she-crab soup in Charleston. *From the author.*

published, but Everett doesn't necessarily think it makes all the difference. Instead, he says most places around town tend to make the soup too thick. Some people also warn that yellow spots in a restaurant's soup may be a shortcut of egg yolks instead of crab roe. Regardless, Everett says he would rather have the kind he makes at home in a big batch once or twice a year. I'm sure most of us would rather try that recipe too.

After the war, Presson and his wife spent some time in Charlotte, North Carolina, even opening a restaurant called the Boar's Head. But as most of us know, there's no place that can quite compare to Charleston, and they eventually found their way back to the coast. Presson made even more connections around town during his time managing the Carolina Yacht Club until he finally built his new restaurant on Cannon Street. Presson's son recalls his mother claiming it was the first building in Charleston to be built for the sole purpose of being a restaurant. Everett's Restaurant officially opened on Cannon Street in 1951. This was an area that was still considered the outskirts of town, near the Ashley River Bridge.

The she-crab soup eventually became so popular at Everett's that they were selling ten gallons a day for takeout and twelve gallons in the restaurant. People would drive from Atlanta and Charlotte, and they would ship it to New York and even Washington, D.C., on an air force plane. In the 1950s, Presson added a room in his restaurant that was dedicated to William Deas. He also placed a neon sign in the front of the restaurant that beckoned, "Try our famous she-crab soup."

Presson was quick to admit that it was Deas who made his restaurant popular, and he tried his best to promote his soup while giving appropriate credit. This was something of a habit of Everett Presson—making sure people were acknowledged for their hard work. Presson's son recalls how his father taught him to value the people who worked for them because they might be working harder than anyone else. His father also taught him to treat customers with respect and recalls him saying, "They could have gone anywhere else, but they came here."

Toward the end of his career, Presson had to make Deas a waiter because so many people came to the restaurant just to see him. He was far too valuable of an employee to stick back in the kitchen anyway. He likely made much more money in the new position due to his following. As a testament to the popularity of Deas's soup, in an interview in 1989, Presson's son explained, "I still run into people today who said the best she-crab soup they ever had was right there at Everett's."[95]

Advertisement for Everett's Restaurant from 1955. *From Nelsons' Charleston City Directory, 1955.*

But it wasn't just the soup that made Everett's so successful. It also had a talking mynah bird that could often be heard asking, "Do you play golf?" When the weather was nice, customers could find Romeo outside as a sort of mascot for the restaurant. However, back when Highway 17 was a smaller two-lane highway, the bird managed to cause a bit of trouble. A man and his lady happened to drive by the restaurant in a convertible right when Romeo let out his classic wolf whistle. In a practically cartoonish case of mistaken identity, the man stormed up to an employee who was outside cleaning the cage, ready to fight the wrong person. Thankfully, Presson quickly jumped out to his employee's defense.

A bit of a troublemaker in more than one way, the bird also picked up some foul language over the years. Waiters who didn't know how to read or write would often call out orders in a very select shorthand that might have increased Romeo's profane vocabulary. Regardless, people would frequently visit Everett's to see the bird. Presson's son even joked that the bird had sent him to college.

In the 1960s, the restaurant suffered major losses, with the passing of William Deas in 1961 and Everett Presson in 1965. Presson's wife carried on the restaurant for a few years but eventually felt the burnout from endless hours of hard work. Everett's Restaurant officially closed in 1969, and Presson's son made a conscious choice to stay out of the restaurant business. "I saw how hard my parents worked. We only closed one day a year," he said in an interview with the author. But he had the good fortune of a name that carried a positive reputation in the local community, which has served him well as a real estate agent. Everett Presson credits his father for instilling a strong work ethic in him, and it's evident to those around him, as he is still hard at work into his seventies.

FINE DINING EMERGES

The quest for a fine dining meal used to require a plane ticket out of Charleston. With such limited choices, it took bold restauranteurs to offer higher-quality dining options downtown. For a lucky few, their efforts were rewarded with reputations that are still held in high regard today.

The Colony House and The Wine Cellar

In a restaurant review in the *Post and Courier* in 1991, Jane Kronsberg started her piece with the bold generalization that "The Colony House has been in existence forever," which, to be fair, is a pretty accurate summation of this restaurant's place within Charleston's culinary history.[96]

The actual beginnings of the restaurant can be traced back to William "Bill" Snipes, who opened a lounge and buffet within the Sergeant Jasper Apartment building in 1952. Snipes had moved into the new apartments after living in Columbia, where he had previously owned a restaurant. He struck up a friendship with J.C. Long, who had built the Sergeant Jasper building, and took advantage of the "ideal restaurant site" that was advertised within the space. The Sergeant Lounge was the first incarnation of a Charleston restaurant legacy.

In the air-conditioned space, the Sergeant Lounge hosted an all-you-can-eat, ninety-cent lunch buffet of meat, salad and vegetables. In the evenings, it offered the house specialty of U.S. prime steak with french fries, salad and rolls for $2.25. In fact, a 1953 advertisement claimed that the lounge sold more steaks than anywhere else in Charleston. This wasn't a surprise to Bill's

"The Colony House" was the winning entry from Bill Snipes's naming contest. *From Ginny Snipes.*

The Sergeant

Lounge and Buffet

CHARLESTON, SOUTH CAROLINA

Left: Menu from the Sergeant Jasper Lounge and Buffet. *From Ginny Snipes.*

Below: Steak was always a feature on the menu of the Sergeant Jasper Lounge and Buffet. *From Ginny Snipes.*

See Our Wine an...

STRIP SIRLOIN
$4.00
served with
French Fries - Salad
Hot Rolls
SERVED EVERY NITE FROM 6 P.M.

(Broiled or Fried)
FRESH FISH (1 lb.)
Potatoes, Special Slaw, Tartar Sauce, Lemon
$1.25

Sergeants' Special . . .

U. S. PRIME
STEAK
Served with
French Fries — Salad — Hot Rolls
$2.25

SEA FOOD DINNER
with
Shrimp, Filet of Flounder, Devil Crab Patties
Tartar Sauce, French Fries and Salad
$1.75

ROAST PRIME RIBS
of BEEF au Jus
Creamed Potatoes, Salad
$2.00

HAWAIIAN
HAM STEAK
Cherry Center
Grilled Pineapple Ring
$1.75

SOUTHERN FRIED CHICKEN
½ Chicken, French Fries
Tossed Green Salad
$1.75

CHEESEBURGER STEAK
Served with
French Fried Potatoes
Lettuce and Tomato Salad
$1.35

OYSTERS OR JUMBO SHRIMP
EXTRA SELECT
with Tartar Sauce
French Fries, Salad
$1.50

COCKTAILS & APPETIZERS

SHRIMP COCKTAIL	.75
FRESH FRUIT (on ice)	.50
CELERY HEARTS AND OLIVES	.60
SARDINES WITH ONION RINGS	.75
TOMATO JUICE	.20

BEVERAGES

COFFEE, TEA, BUTTERMILK	.10
MILK	.11

SERGEANT'S TOSSED GREEN SALAD BOWL	35c
FRENCH FRIED POTATOES	40c
FRENCH FRIED ONIONS	50c

COMBINATION SANDWICH
(Double Decker)
Ham and Cheese
French Fries — Pickle
75c

90c Buffet Luncheon Served Every Weekday from 12 to 3 P. M.

daughter, Ginny Snipes, who said, "My father thought you should have five steaks a week."[97]

In 1953, the lounge added a dining room and decided to run a contest in the paper to name the space. The naming contest had five judges for the twenty-five-dollar prize (adjusted for inflation, this is a little more than $235 today) and proved to be incredibly popular. More than six thousand names were submitted, forty-nine of which were for The Flag Room, the space's eventual name. Margaret B. Hickey was the lucky winner because her submission was received first.[98]

The name was chosen because of the connections to Sergeant Jasper who heroically replaced the South Carolina flag that was shot down by the British during a Revolutionary War battle on Sullivan's Island. In homage to its namesake, the dining room was decorated with various flags, the tables were adorned with red lamps and white shelves lined the walls. A hardwood dance floor centered the room—an addition that happened to be big news when it was first installed.

When Snipes moved the restaurant to 4 Vendue Range in 1959, he continued the tradition of a naming contest. This time the stakes were a bit higher, as he offered a fifty-dollar cash prize to the winner (worth more than $400 today). The advertisement read:

> *On or about December 1st, The Flag Room is moving to 4 Vendue Range—to become part of a new, larger and finer overall operation, in which will be featured the very best in beverages, steaks, chops and seafoods. At our new address you'll find an atmosphere that reflects with dignity and good taste the period when sailing ships graced the harbor of Charleston and the waterfront of Vendue Range. The management will be the same as at The Flag Room and the Sergeant Jasper Lounge. Too, the same personnel will be on hand: but substantially increased to assure the gracious, efficient service you'll be expecting.*
>
> *We need an appropriate name for the overall operation at 4 Vendue Range. Please help us by entering our name contest.*[99]

According to the contest winner announcement published a few weeks later, Snipes received hundreds of entries with multiple suggestions of "The Colony House," which proved to be the winning name. Once again, due to the large number of submissions, his contest came down to selecting a winner with the earliest post mark.

The Flag Room at the Sergeant Jasper. *From Ginny Snipes.*

The first incarnation of The Colony House was located at 4 Vendue Range. *From Ginny Snipes.*

The dining room of The Colony House at 4 Vendue Range. *From Ginny Snipes.*

At the Vendue Range location, The Colony House had an open dining area and smaller dining rooms. The Flag Room dining area continued the legacy already established in the Sergeant Jasper building and was decorated with the many flags Bill had collected since its opening. The room for the Lords Proprietors provided an homage to the founders of Charleston. These dining rooms would remain a steadfast tradition within The Colony House, even as it continued to grow and move around the city. With impressive eyes for detail, Snipes and his wife even traveled to London to secure the paintings of the proprietors that they would use in their dining rooms. In a letter from May 1967, developer J.C. Long wrote to Snipes congratulating him and his wife, Ruth, on their achievement at Vendue Range, noting how far the restaurant had come since its Sergeant Jasper days. Vendue Range would be home to The Colony House for another ten years before making its last, and most drastic, move.

The Room of the Seven Lords within The Colony House. *From Ginny Snipes.*

The Flag Room remained a part of The Colony House. *From Ginny Snipes.*

The Colony House's final home was more than eighteen thousand square feet of old coffee warehouse space from the early 1800s. Snipes had to have vision and forethought at the time, considering the status of the building and surrounding area. He invested eight months and $500,000 to open The Colony House as it is most recently remembered. The massive space was created in anticipation of possibly doubling the business, with seating for five hundred people and a kitchen that was four times larger than the Vendue Range space. The original tie beams, arches and brick were left as they were, and the interior was black, red, green and gold, with handmade Mexican benches and antique guns hung over the doorways.

There were three dining rooms on the first floor that showcased original pine trusses and Tiffany lead glass fixtures. The second floor held two banquet rooms, while the third floor housed business offices and a terrace overlooking the Charleston Harbor. Snipes had hoped that the third-floor terrace would be popular for the sweeping views of the harbor back before parking garages, private residences and Waterfront Park blocked the view on Prioleau Street. However, his daughter Ginny recalls that outdoor dining in the Charleston heat never really caught on as he had hoped.

Bill Snipes's advertisement promoting the new location of The Colony House. *From Ginny Snipes.*

The finished building was described in detail by travel magazines, stating that it "echoes a time when tall sailing ships arrived in the harbor with French wines or Brazilian coffee, then departed with cargoes of rice and cotton."[100] While the Snipeses had established their restaurant as one of the ultimate fine dining spots in town, the only issue with its location on the harbor and a name like The Colony House was that people often showed up with their bags thinking it could be their hotel as well.

The city took notice of the building's transformation. Snipes's old friend J.C. Long sent a letter in 1979 stating that Snipes had given Charleston something to be proud of. But it wasn't just friends and supporters who took notice—local historical societies were impressed as well. Snipes received letters from Elizabeth Jenkins Young, president of the Preservation Society of Charleston, and Mrs. S. Henry Edmunds, director of the Historic Charleston Foundation. Their letters thanked him for choosing to restore an old warehouse instead of building something more "modern."

The restaurant was frequented by politicians, local business owners and tourists alike. The family's scrapbook collection included thank-you letters from representatives, invitations to the governor's mansion and many more accolades. It was a place where couples held wedding receptions, got engaged

Crews turned an abandoned warehouse into The Colony House on Prioleau Street. *From Ginny Snipes.*

The final location of The Colony House at 35 Prioleau Street. *From Ginny Snipes.*

and celebrated anniversaries. The collection of memories was a testament to the good times and great service people found at The Colony House.

The menu was described as "southern hospitality with a Lowcountry accent"[101] and advertised that it was "home of the she-crab soup and famous for charcoal steaks and Charleston seafoods."[102] In an interview with local chef Robert Dickson in 2016, he stated that The Colony House was "THE original fine dining restaurant in Charleston."[103]

A collection of menus from 1980 offered a more detailed look at the offerings. Appetizers included shrimp various ways, oysters, scallops, escargot and even an onion pie. If guests selected the "authentic low country dinner," they would receive a choice of Carolina onion pie or she-crab soup, salad and Lowcountry chicken and shrimp creole with Carolina rice. Dessert would include "Charlotte's lemon cup custard." This was all for twelve dollars.[104]

When Snipes was ready retire in 1976, he first offered the business to his daughter, Ginny. She was a junior in college around that time and adamantly declined, acutely aware of how much time and energy goes into running a restaurant. She stated that even though they had a lot of great people who helped the family run The Colony House, they still found themselves there all the time.

At that point, Snipes sold the business to the team of Franz Meier, Chris Weihs and Harry Waddington. They brought a new perspective to the already established fine dining scene and wanted to continue to up the stakes. Meier recalls that when he bought The Colony House, there just weren't that many restaurants in Charleston. They introduced a new menu with imported foods over the more traditional southern dishes, admitting that they wanted to show the people of Charleston that there were other ways to eat. Even though they made quite a few changes, the new team decided to keep a hamburger on the menu out of necessity, but they did have to raise the price by twenty-five cents.

The people of Charleston weren't necessarily welcoming to the changes at their established restaurant, and business dropped in response to the unfamiliar cuisine. Meier was quoted as saying, "We had a revolution on our hands," in reference to those early days of ownership.[105] So they went back to the old menu but decided on a new strategy with perhaps a slower introduction to change and European influence. To approach this, they opened The Wine Cellar within The Colony House in 1977.

The Wine Cellar was a restaurant within a restaurant—a way to incorporate a rarely used lunchroom that Meier described as "the ugliest in America." The humble beginnings of the space made the transformation that much more impressive, as it eventually became a fine dining room dedicated to French cuisine and boasted an extensive wine list.

Hiding behind a heavy door in the corner, the cozy, quiet space could accommodate up to fifty people, but the team mostly focused on serving around forty at a time. The scene was described as a comfortable wine cellar with linen tablecloths and candlelight dining. The service was excellent amid the floor-to-ceiling wine racks that lined the brick walls as a way to provide both ambiance and seclusion.

Advertisements for The Colony House and The Wine Cellar from 1984. *From* On The Towne *vol. 3, 1984.*

Chef Roland Henin brought his authentic French cuisine to The Wine Cellar. Entrées could include jumbo shrimp Provençale, côte de veau London House, roast rack of lamb Persillade and Tournedos Charleston. Salad was served after the entrée in true European fashion, while cherries jubilee or bananas foster graced the dessert list. In the beginning, the restaurant didn't even have written menus, and the maître d'hôtel would announce the offerings when the guests sat down. The produce was so fresh, the menu often wasn't posted until the late afternoon anyway.

A customer could even choose six to ten bottles of his favorite wine and keep them in place on a special rack with an engraved brass nameplate—one way to ensure his favorite was always available. The stellar reputation of the restaurant grew through word of mouth, and the very existence of The Wine Cellar significantly upped the standard of dining in Charleston. Whereas Charlestonians used to have to fly to New York City to get a nice meal, they could now find a culinary delight right in their backyard.

The new business owners' strategy certainly paid off, as the European, and specifically French, influence continued to widen downtown. The 1970s were a time of expansion in tastes and visitors to the city, which was largely impacted by the introduction of the Spoleto arts festival.

A final change in ownership occurred in 1990, when Dick Elliott took over. He was an unlikely candidate, as he had previously been a lawyer and corporate executive and had no restaurant ownership experience. But this was a new era in Charleston. A restaurant wasn't just a passion project but a business investment, and Elliott saw an opportunity to invest in a promising business based on a recommendation he received from Charleston culinary legend Louis Osteen.[106]

Regardless of his background, Elliott worked hard to continue the established reputation of The Colony House within the community, because when a restaurant has been successfully serving generations of Charlestonians, continuity is key. Classics like crab cakes continued to be served, but the Elliotts added a few more elements, such as artwork from local artists, poetry readings, dinner theater, book signings and even concerts. They also founded an annual fundraising event for the local arts council.

While looking toward the future, Elliott also kept an eye on the past and stayed in touch with Bill Snipes's wife, Ruth. With her input, they were able to maintain some aspects of the restaurant as they always had been. While it had to be a bit surreal to watch things change, Ginny Snipes acknowledged that change was inevitable when it came to adjusting to the city's growing tourism scene.

Not too long after gaining ownership of The Colony House, Elliott teamed up with a local chef named Frank Lee. In an almost classic Charleston culinary tale, Elliott has described first seeing Lee unloading fresh produce and meat from across the street.[107] Lee was a pioneer in locally sourced, fresh ingredients, and Elliott knew he was someone he wanted to work with.

Elliott and Lee were an excellent match, so much so that they decided to open something different together. Their new restaurant would be less formal, leaning away from special event dining. Unfortunately, that also meant the end for The Colony House, which had its last service on November 28, 1993. The closure of this restaurant opened the door for another classic, Slightly North of Broad (SNOB), to open shortly after.

The Colony House was remembered for its significant place in Charleston's history. "It's an old Charleston institution, and we have some fond memories there," patron Vito Scarafile said in 1993.[108] Another local woman who grew up eating there had a more promising premonition, "It will be back, one day The Colony House will be back."[109] The building still sits on a much more confined Prioleau Street—tucked away almost like a forgotten gem. The space was purchased by the Harbour Club, which still operates there today.

Perdita's

Perdita's was another restaurant that helped pave the way for fine dining in Charleston. In fact, it was fine dining before fine dining really even existed in this city. Often described as both the queen and mother of fine dining in Charleston, this restaurant set a precedent that won't soon be forgotten.

Gordon W. Bennett, from "up north" in Massachusetts, opened Perdita's in 1953. He had settled in Charleston after serving in the U.S. Army Air Corps during World War II and decided to start a restaurant with an intimate, stylish dining room at 10 Exchange Street.

Bennett chose the name Perdita's based on Charleston folklore. Mrs. Paul Robinson, an actress famous for her portrayal of Perdita in Shakespeare's *Winter's Tale*, supposedly incited a mortal duel between two men on Meeting Street over her performance. A copy of Gainsborough's painting of her hung in the dining room in reference to this connection.

In a city that often hears a few tour guide embellishments, an article in the local paper in 1968 was quick to clear up the details of this story. While Mrs. Robinson was a frequent visitor to the city, and had indeed performed at the Dock Street Theatre, the duel was supposedly in reference to another woman's performance.[110] Regardless, people were likely to let the whole thing slide for this particular establishment.

The building's history added a feeling of age and establishment to the new restaurant. Two-foot-thick brick walls dated back to the Revolutionary War, and a cast-iron balcony added carefully designed details to the spot that was originally a cotton exchange. Candlelight, chandeliers and exposed-brick walls inside added a comfortable and elegant ambiance that was supported by a commitment to service and attention to detail. Guests would feel important and pampered without too much pretension—as long as they didn't find finger bowls with twists of lemon too formal.

The handwritten menu, which changed nightly, highlighted French cuisine while also taking advantage of local seafood. Fruits de la Mer became synonymous with Perdita's. Once described as a "luxury class seafood platter,"[111] it could contain items such as baked crabmeat Remick, local flounder, roast oysters, lobster dainties and the tail of a puffer fish (also known as sea squab). Other staples on the menu included escargot, Chateaubriand, foie gras and truffles and Roast Oysters Perdita. Charleston classic she-crab soup was served with sherry poured from a brandy snifter, and little fried mashed potato balls were served with applesauce in a combination that just seemed to work.

It didn't take long for Perdita's to build a reputation for gourmet dining. Within three years, it won *Holiday* magazine's certificate for "dining distinction as one of the outstanding restaurants in the United States," and Charleston was the only city on the East Coast between New York and Miami to earn such a distinction. In reference to the award, a member of the magazine staff noted, "It is given because somewhere in the operation there is personality, creativeness, and individuality which deserves recognition."[112]

The awards and celebration continued, and in 1960, Perdita's was awarded the "Council of Paris Medal of Honor," a distinction awarded to only five restaurants in the entire country. The award hung proudly in the dining room at a time when restaurant awards were a big deal for Charleston, as they helped bring awareness to the city and its culinary scene.

The restaurant's popularity grew by leaps and bounds, as did its size. In 1967, Perdita's underwent a $50,000 expansion to add two private dining rooms, two new restrooms, a walk-in wine cellar and a kitchen four times its original size. Overall, the expansion added fifty new seats. The three-thousand-square-foot addition was described in a 1967 news article as "decorated partially in red velvet, exposed brick and beams and a wainscoting around the floor to a height of about three feet and partially with a Spanish motif to include tiled floors and Moorish emblazenments."[113]

Continued exposure on a national platform helped thrust Charleston into the dining spotlight. A Perdita's feature in *Southern Living* in 1968 was covered in the local papers and was lauded as "the sort of publicity that's bound to draw crowds."[114] Perdita's became so popular that the owners even had to run an advertisement in the papers in 1968 to clarify that it wasn't affiliated with any other restaurant trying to mooch off its reputation.[115]

The waiters were attentive and offered exquisite service and even wore diamond pins to designate their years of service, which could reach decades. Everything about the restaurant was a symbol of established glory and high standards. Alas, an untouchable reputation is always difficult to maintain. Diners entered with such high expectations that anything below excellent was practically intolerable. When local reporter Frank Jarrell dined there in 1979, he felt as if the Perdita's of the past was gone. With what he described as overcooked scallops, bland flavors and fatty meat, he left the meal "greatly disappointed—even angry."[116]

In that same year, a contributing editor to the *International Review of Food and Wine* commented that her Gem Island chicken and oyster pie was "the most gruesome combination that could ever have been put together."[117] But even when the food was good, it just didn't seem to be enough to match the high price point. And in the early '80s, locals feared that the restaurant had declined to "only a musty shadow of its former self," as Frank Jarrell recalled in a 1989 review of the restaurant that replaced Perdita's.[118]

The restaurant was closed by 1986, and the many advertisements announcing the auction of the restaurant equipment were a sad sendoff of what was once a culinary giant. However, Perdita's story wasn't over with the closure. The building was leased by new owners, who would eventually pay homage to one of Charleston's original fine dining restaurants with the start of their own lost restaurant, Carolina's.

COMMUNITY GATHERING PLACES

While restaurants like Perdita's were busy increasing Charleston's reputation for fine dining, other establishments had their own unique purposes. Locals appreciated the familiarity of a regular lunch spot, the comfort of hearty family dinners or just a place to connect with their neighbors.

Some of these restaurants even provided an important backdrop for the community to spark change and progress. At a time when segregation determined who could eat where, local restaurants provided opportunities for people to gather and create a sense of community. This was especially true in Charleston during the civil rights movement. Our city hosted a visit from Martin Luther King Jr. in 1967 and was the scene of the influential hospital strikes of 1969. There were curfews and tension in the city, which greatly impacted everyone's daily lives.

The following restaurants are strong examples of the importance of community gathering places and how a building can hold so much more purpose than what is advertised on the outside. An intricate part of Charleston's unique character, these are the kinds of places that people might remember for the food, but more likely for the people who worked and gathered there—those who made everyone feel like family.

Freida's

Freida's was always described as having a family feel, which could have been due to the family who ran it. The restaurant began as a spaghetti house in the 1950s, which meant it had a focus on a few crowd pleasers, such as pasta, lasagna and pizza. The setting in an old house on Society Street also helped create that homey feel with flowerpots on the entryway and walls, and the main dining room was set up right in the front room of the house.

Since the restaurant closed by eight or nine in the evening, it was usually the perfect spot for an early dinner. The clientele included both locals and tourists, brought together over a comfortable atmosphere and reasonable prices. College students were also attracted to the casual, home-cooked offerings—including a lasagna the size of an entire dinner plate—that reminded them of home.

Perhaps more notable than the food was Gus, who was known as Grandpa or just Papa to some. Retired from his career driving trucks, he still found himself at work in his family's restaurant. Although he considered himself to just be "helping out," he would seat guests, run the register and interact with the customers.[119] Walking down from his apartment above the restaurant, he seemed more than happy to assume his duties on a daily basis. Gus was famous for charming guests, offering a chocolate kiss on Valentine's Day and maybe just a banana or mint any other day. He offered a familiar, comforting laugh from behind the register as his daughters, Freida and Elaine, ran the restaurant.

Upon the sad news of Gus's passing in 1989, people in the community remembered him fondly. Sharon E. Frazier, a former Freida's employee, wrote to the paper, "I think as many people came to Freida's for his jokes and kind words as they did for the excellent food Elaine and Freida prepared."[120] While the restaurant eventually became Cafe Society, and is now home to Muse, most will fondly remember the home of Freida's.

The Patio Famous Tea Room

The Patio Famous Tea Room was named appropriately because it didn't even seem to need the faded sign above the door. A neighborhood restaurant in Elliotborough, it was opened in 1962 by Mary Campbell McKnight, otherwise known as "Miss Mary."[121] Her loyal mix of customers represented the local community.

Miss Mary provided a lot of food for a reasonable price. The menu was handwritten and changed daily. It included down-home, soul-food staples such as fried fish, stewed chicken, red rice, okra soup, corn bread and Miss Mary's famous bread pudding. For breakfast, customers could even find grits or fried bologna.

Mary eventually gave up management of the restaurant to Alluette Jones Smalls. When the restaurant closed in the 1990s, it sat vacant until the renovation and subsequent opening of Trattoria Lucca in 2008. Alluette, however, went on to run Alluette's Cafe and Alluette's Jazz Cafe on Reid and Calhoun Streets, respectively. Her restaurant was featured on BBC America's *Million Dollar Critic* television show, where she won the competition with her holistic soul food that stood out even without the use of pork or sugar. Her cuisine offered highly rated organic dishes, such as lima bean soup, that were always worth the wait. Even with her success and recognition, her restaurant closed in 2014.

Kitty's Fine Foods

As NoMo around North Morrison Street was once called the Auto Mile, 1137 Morrison Drive was once home to Kitty's Fine Foods.

Neeley Katherine "Kitty" Proctor and her husband, Tom, were married in 1948 and moved to Charleston after he was transferred with his ice company. Since the industry was on its way out, Tom decided to get into the restaurant business and took over Hunley's Soda Fountain at 286 King Street and later the O.K. Diner on Morrison in 1963. Tom didn't like it much on Morrison Street, so Kitty took over. She renovated the place and opened it under the name Kitty's Fine Foods.

Kitty had been a bank teller since the age of sixteen, so her high perch on the stool behind the register was both comfortable and familiar. She operated with her own enthusiasm but also with sage advice given to her by Sullivan's Island businessman "Chip" Anderegg. Kitty remembered his wise words, "If anyone provided good food and was nice to the customers, the world would beat a path to the restaurant even if it were in the middle of the ocean."[122]

Kitty's attitude about business set the tone for decades of dining at her restaurant. She was the kind of person who couldn't be forced into a bad day. She wasn't even angry when her purse was ripped from her hands one day while leaving the restaurant, instead she simply referred to it as one of those lessons in life. She even made a joke about opening a drive-in restaurant when someone plowed a car straight into her front window. "I don't believe in getting upset. My advice is to be concerned if you can do something about it," she explained in an interview in 1976.[123] Kitty possessed an infectious enthusiasm that she attempted to project onto others, whether through the motivational signs posted on her cash register or her "thought for the day" advice printed on her menus.

With an owner like Kitty, guests could become regulars after the first visit, but many came to see her every day, including a group of local businessmen who earned the reliable title of the "9:15 Coffee Club." The group even brought in their own long maple butcher block table to gather around. The surroundings at Kitty's included an eclectic mix of tables, chairs and booths, with wood paneling on the wall and, of course, a simple, yet prominent cat theme.

Regardless of the surroundings, the focus at Kitty's was always the food and the customers. An eclectic mix of tradesmen, businessmen, lawyers, doctors and members of the clergy would come from all over the city for a meal. Kitty greeted every single person who came into her restaurant and held her staff to the same expectations. This sort of familiarity with the customers would become necessary training because her customers were the type to call and ask for the usual without even identifying themselves. Regardless, Miss Kitty would always have a regular customer's order ready because she always knew who came in at what time.

The menu was only for breakfast and lunch, as Kitty's closed promptly at three in the afternoon. The dining experience wasn't fancy, but even when it came served on a plastic plate, guests could count on it being delicious. While there were specials named after regular customers like the "Red Dempsey" (a hamburger with peppers, onions and hot sauce created for a car salesman who used to work next door), Kitty's was widely known for the meat and two—or the meat and three, depending on how hungry customers were. Meat options regularly included baked ham, fried chicken, fried flounder, grilled salmon, smoked sausage and country cube steak. The combinations were endless when paired with fifteen different vegetable sides, although Kitty's fried squash was difficult to match anywhere else around town. If guests could handle a biscuit too, they'd be in for a treat, especially if they washed it all down with a refreshing iced tea.

In the late 1980s, Kitty was ready to retire, which is when she met David Runey. She gave him the opportunity to run the restaurant for two months before he decided to buy it, since she was not one to rush an important decision. David decided to take the opportunity and continued the well-established tradition of putting the customer first. He was careful not to change what Kitty had created, which included keeping the cat decor in the restaurant, though no one would ever love cats quite as much as Kitty. When she had officially retired, Kitty would still stop in and sit behind the cash register, ensuring a smooth transition to a new owner.

Runey ran the business for many years, until it changed hands once again in 2006, and Martha Grant took over. She made some changes, rebranding the restaurant as Kitty's Diner and tweaking a few of the menu items. Down-home cooking remained the focus, with daily specials like BBQ day, beef liver and onions or meatloaf with okra soup. This final change of ownership was a bit more difficult on the business, and Grant had some trouble regaining clientele. The building on Meeting Street was sold one final time in 2009 to Jen and Mike Kulick, who took the establishment down to the studs, traded in cat decor for a moose head and rebuilt it as the Tattooed Moose.

Ladson House

Sitting at the corner of President and Kennedy Streets was the Ladson House. The restaurant was a dream come true for Edward D. "Eddie" Ladson, who wanted to own his own place after working for thirty-seven years as a chief steward at the Charleston Yacht Club. During that time, Ladson learned a lot about quality food, especially working under Gordon Bennett, the founder of Perdita's.

He was fully supported by the community in his venture to provide a decent place to eat in the neighborhood. "At the time, there was no high-class place for black people to go," Ladson said in an interview in 1981.[124] He had quite a few hoops to jump through to offer such a place, including rezoning the area for business and securing the $25,000 he needed to get it officially up and running in 1963.[125]

Ladson had the bright pink Flamingo Room and a larger wood-paneled Presidente Room for hosting celebrations and banquets. These rooms also provided an important backdrop for the many political meetings held at the Ladson House, which quickly became an epicenter for the black community. Politicians and business owners would frequently gather there, especially in the days of segregation when they weren't welcome in other establishments. Charleston councilman Wendell Gilliard stated in a 2004 interview that "If you were running for political office, you had to come here and tell the black community your plans."[126]

A Ladson House advertisement from 1969 displayed the restaurant's many offerings. *From Hill's Charleston City Directory, 1969.*

The menu featured items like fried flounder, barbecue chicken, ham and beans, pork chops and okra soup. The restaurant also offered desserts, such as bread pudding, banana pudding and pound cake, as well as a complete soda fountain and ice cream service. A signature dessert of the Ladson House was called the Flamingo Royal, which was created by Alice Warren. The decadent dish consisted of chocolate cake and vanilla ice cream with fudge, crème de menthe and a cherry on top.

Desegregation caused an interesting predicament for the restaurant because then, as Ladson said in 1981, "All of a sudden I was competing against every white restaurant in the community."[127] But there was also a rise in crime in the area, which deterred business, especially in the evening hours.

A heart attack forced Ladson to slow down, and he retired in 1981. At that time, he passed the day-to-day management to Alice Warren, who had worked there for thirteen years. Unfortunately, the writing was already on the wall for the business, as the Ladson House closed for good in 1985. But that wouldn't be the end of the restaurant's legacy. The Ladson House spawned other legends of the kitchen, including Alice Warren, who went on to open Alice's Restaurant, and Martha Lou Gadsden, who opened Martha Lou's Kitchen in 1983.

However, as the life force of this particular business moved on to other ventures, the building sat boarded up and falling apart for years to follow. A sad shell of what was once a prominent focal point in the community, the plan was to turn the building into a community center and restore it as an important site in the area.

Brooks Restaurant

While Brooks Restaurant may have had its official opening in January 1967, the family restaurant business had already been buzzing since the 1930s. In 1934, Henry Brooks opened a small café in town, which would be the jumping-off point of what would be an incredibly successful family business.

Henry had two younger brothers, Albert and Benjamin, and together they also owned the Brooks Pool Room on Morris Street. Their businesses were successful, and even offered the opportunity to send Albert to college at Allen University. He completed two years of school before he went off to Europe to serve in World War II, where he became a first sergeant in the United States Army. During his time in the military, Albert would write back to the local papers describing his interactions with different black soldiers and the quest for equal treatment after risking their lives in the military—an experience that may have driven him toward future success.

When he returned from war in 1946, Albert's intention was to complete his degree. But when his brothers Henry and Benjamin asked for help upon his return, he obliged. Those brothers had used the profits from their restaurant business to send him to school in the first place, so Albert felt that it was only right to offer his help when asked. While still a difficult decision, Albert was aided in his choice by the advice of his mentor, Dr. Higgins. Dr. Higgins was the president of Allen University, but also Albert's principal from both elementary and high school. His guidance inspired Albert to go home and help his brothers because he could still continue his education through traveling, talking to people and reading. Dr. Higgins told him, "You may not ever get a college degree, but you will be just as educated as anybody who has one."[128]

Albert continued this focus on real-world education and was always willing to learn from any opportunity. In 1948, he stood on the street to survey the walking and driving traffic on Morris Street and came to the conclusion that a restaurant would do well in that particular location. Less than a year later, Albert and his brothers turned the Pool Room into a restaurant called Brooks Grill.

Albert eventually went to New York University in 1960 to study real estate. This led to additional ventures, including a real estate company and, around 1963, a motel. As some of the only places black leaders could stay when in town, both the Brooks Motel and Brooks Grill were central to the civil rights movement in Charleston. Hundreds of people would gather in his restaurant for political meetings, including the organization

BROOKS MOTEL AND RESTAURANT

CHARLESTON'S FINEST
MOTEL and RESTAURANT

SEA FOODS
STEAKS and
FRIED CHICKEN

EXCELLENT MOTEL
ACCOMODATIONS
FINE FOODS

FELIX AT MORRIS ST.   TELS. (803) 723-9264 - 65 - 66 722-6685

Brooks Motel and Restaurant advertisements from 1972. *From Hill's Charleston City Directory, 1972.*

of the United Citizens Party. This sentiment of community gathering continued when the Brooks Restaurant officially opened its doors in 1967 and was billed as "a restaurant for everyone" in its advertisement in the local paper.[129]

However, the events in the city and the country were still apparent when Joe Falls, a sports editor from Detroit, came to town to see Cassius Clay in the summer of 1970. After working up the courage to walk inside, he was painfully aware of the fact that he was the only white man in the restaurant. But it appeared that no one else seemed to bat an eye as he reported, "I could have been green for all they cared. I was there for the same reason they were: to get some lunch."[130] He enjoyed his steak sandwich with an appreciation for the pleasant Charleston experience, even though he wrongfully assumed all of those Brooks businesses on Morris Street must have been owned by a white man.

Albert Brooks said that he, too, eventually felt the financial side effects of desegregation, and the novelty of being able to enter a once white-only place of business hurt their bottom line. The change was welcome, just an ironic side effect of progress. Albert felt the economic impact across all of his businesses and even set his room prices below the other hotels to remain competitive. However, the restaurant closed down in 1979.

Albert continued to live the example of the value of learning through experiences. He was assertive to ask for help when he needed it—whether to secure financing or business advice. He focused on doing everything well, which seemed to simply attract more success. He never really displayed his wealth either but was described as a modest and hardworking man. Beyond the establishments he brought to Charleston, Albert also formed the Veteran Civic Organization and helped open typically white-only facilities to hosting black community functions. With his many accomplishments,

Albert could have easily moved anywhere in the world, but as he said in an interview in 1967, "I like it here in my hometown of Charleston. I have done well here, I have prospered."[131] A feat of hard work for which Charleston owes him a debt of gratitude.

CONVERTED SPACES

Charleston's architecture is a large part of our city's overall charm. A skyline of church steeples reflects both the beauty and history of our city. It was only a matter of time until the growth of the culinary industry overflowed into some of these spaces with unique concepts.

The Chapel Market Place

Sailors wishing to worship during their time in Charleston's port used to have to attend Bethel on Meeting Street. However, when the location of the church was determined to be inconvenient to the sailors, the city needed a new plan. The corner of East Bay and Market Streets used to be known as Cotesworth Square, as it was the site of General Charles Cotesworth Pinckney's home. The plot of land bequeathed from Ms. Harriott Pinckney was reserved for the purpose of creating a church where visiting seamen could worship and proved to be the perfect spot for development.

After a $35,000 investment, the groundbreaking for the Episcopal Church of the Redeemer began in 1915.[132] The church wasn't just a place of worship, but it also had a passageway that connected the chapel to a social building and home known as the Harriott Pinckney Home for Seamen.

Finished and consecrated in the spring of 1916, sailors had the opportunity to rent a bed in the dormitories for twenty-five cents. The advertisements offered amenities such as a bathroom, breakfast, telephone in the lobby, reading room and game room. While popular at the time, the home eventually became obsolete when sailors stayed in port for shorter amounts of time or were willing to shell out more money for an actual hotel room. Because of this decline in business, the church was deconsecrated in 1964 and was eventually placed on the market.

In 1966, it was announced that the church would be used for a restaurant, and the community was reassured that it would maintain the tranquil

The Seamen's Chapel has been home to many restaurants since it was deconsecrated in 1964. *From the author.*

atmosphere of its former role. Wilbur Burbage and Foy Parker, two former managers of Perdita's restaurant, took over the lease. Chapel Market Place opened with seating for 150 people as well as accommodations in the seamen's home for another 75. Many of the religious symbols were removed, but they kept most features of the original church, such as the heart of pine vaulted ceiling and the twenty-five-foot stained-glass window. The room to the left of the sanctuary became home to a wine cellar, and the pulpit, made of a ship's bow, became a serving station. The renovation from church to modern restaurant cost around $40,000.[133]

Chapel Market Place specialized in French cuisine and became one of the elite fine dining restaurants in the city. In an article featured in the *New York Times* in 1967, the reviewer compared Chapel Market Place to Perdita's, and the steaks and lobster tails were highly recommended.[134] When critic Frank Jarrell dined there in 1980, he tried options such as the escargot, oysters Gino and steak Diane and observed that the cherries jubilee were flambéed right from the pulpit.[135] The restaurant was featured in *Life* magazine in 1969 and received an award from *Esquire* magazine in 1970—a distinction given to only thirty-eight restaurants in the country.

When the owner retired in 1983, the loss of Chapel Market Place opened the door for several other restaurants to fill the space. Ferante's arrived in 1983, which later became Catch 32 and the Art Deco space of L.A. Grill after Hurricane Hugo renovations. Mesa Grill took up residency in the early 1990s, and then Papillon moved from across the street. Many people remember the space as the party bar Mad River Bar and Grill, which allowed people to get drunk in a church until two in the morning for nearly nine years.

The building's current occupant, 5Church, took over in 2015, with Jamie Lynch as the restaurant's executive chef and partner. While the name seemed convenient for the building, the business was actually an expansion from the brand's original Charlotte, North Carolina location. Chef Lynch went on to compete in season fourteen of the Bravo television show *Top Chef*, which just happened to be filmed in Charleston in 2016. As one of the smallest cities to host the culinary competition, Charleston's reputation for culinary excellence was proudly on national display. Now, 5Church remains a stand-out dining experience in the market area, and with the entirety of Sun Tzu's *The Art of War* scrawled on the ceiling of a former place of worship, the restaurant offers a refined dining atmosphere but doesn't take itself too seriously.

SCARLETT O'HARA

Some restaurants last for decades, while others don't need that long to make an impression on this city. The Scarlett O'Hara earned a place among the lost restaurants of Charleston for its unique concept: a floating barge turned restaurant.

The barge was originally called the *Andros Mariner*, complete at 215 feet long and thirty-six feet wide. The vessel was built in 1921 as a Great Lakes steamer and then enlarged as an oceangoing vessel in 1950.[136] William Shields and Susan L. Drew were partners in the project to transform the ship to a restaurant. They were able to purchase the barge at a sheriff's sale and renovate it to resemble a Civil War blockade runner. It mirrored the long, low profile of the "fast steamers" that were able to get by the blockading Union navy at the entrance to the Charleston Harbor during the Civil War.

The vessel had only eight thousand square feet of floor space. They laid reinforced concrete into the hull to create the floor, which weighed it down to a hefty one thousand tons. The outside was painted white, which mimicked similar ships that attempted to avoid Union forces in the daylight during the war.

The restaurant was moored at the Town Creek Boat Yard at the foot of Charlotte Street, and its address was technically Charlotte Street at the

Cooper River when it opened in 1974. The press focused on promoting the restaurant's fire-retardant materials, extinguishers and the many available exits, as a fire on a vessel seemed like the most likely concern at the time.

The decor was elegant within the tight quarters. Chandeliers, green velvet curtains and nautical brass fixtures all added a classy touch, while the grand staircase led to the lounge and dining room. Paintings of Rhett Butler and his lady graced the walls, which was appropriate considering the restaurant was named in reference to *Gone with the Wind*.

The restaurant was split into three areas: the Cargo Hold for dancing, the Paddle Wheel for drinking or happy hour and the Nassau Dining room for indulging in "continental American" meals with specials like coquilles St.-Jacques and oysters Mornay. A visit to the Scarlett O'Hara wasn't simply for a meal; it was an experience of drinks and entertainment.

In September 1975, a two-hundred-foot barge got loose from a line in high winds and bumped the Scarlett O'Hara a few times on the stern after colliding with a dolphin. This caused only minor damage and minimal interruption to dinner service, as a quick-thinking employee tethered the barge to the restaurant to mitigate any further damage.[137]

The novelty wore off by the end of 1977, and the restaurant closed in December. It appeared that the business wasn't pulling the profit needed to maintain such an elaborate operation. But the closure was far from the end of the Scarlett O'Hara's story.

On Sunday, January 28, 1979, the restaurant hit bottom at low tide around 1:30 a.m. and began taking on water as the tide came in.[138] Heavy winds also contributed to the mess, and the Scarlett O'Hara went down. The ship was marked with a buoy since it was mostly underwater, and the surrounding floating debris created a sad sight. It had only been a year since the restaurant had closed.

The sinking, as well as the dredging-up process, was covered closely in the local papers—a morbid progression of a broken, sunken ship. The wreck eventually started moving into the navigation channel of the Charleston Harbor, which could have blocked important marine traffic. The Scarlett O'Hara was stabilized with an appropriately, but depressingly named dead man rig, which required a sixteen-foot pipe sunk in concrete. This procedure cost $6,000.[139]

The week before it sank, the owners had all of the carpets cleaned and the entire ship polished for a prospective buyer. Instead, the restaurant ended with a $324,000 contract just to remove the vessel from the water.[140]

3

An Influx of New Culinary Styles

The culinary scene in Charleston around the 1970s is best described by a phrase repeated multiple times across almost every interview: "There just weren't any restaurants at that time." This recurring opinion has been solidified by the research, but those who only know Charleston as it is today might be surprised by this description. In fact, a restaurant review from 1976 began with the writer stating, "Mention dining out to a Charlestonian and chances are you'll be greeted with a complaint: 'There aren't any decent restaurants in the city.'"[141] Just let that soak in while you desperately try to fit one more meal in your belly before you head back home.

So, what changed between then and now? Perhaps the drastic changes had something to do with a few keen eyes for growth, foresight and revitalization. When Joseph P. Riley Jr. became mayor of the city in 1975 (a position he held for the next forty years), he quickly went to work spearheading change downtown, which included a revitalization of the business district. Around that time, it was also announced that Charleston would host the Spoleto Festival in 1977—an event that is often credited as a turning point in our culinary scene.

The Spoleto Festival, known as the "Festival of Two Worlds," was already a long-running annual event in Spoleto, Italy, and the organizers spent years searching for an American counterpart. Charleston seemed to fit the bill for a city that would be enveloped in the festival and still be able to handle the size of the many different performances, including operas, concerts, dance, poetry and plays. Upon the announcement that Charleston had been selected as the host, the local paper summed up high expectations that "the festival is expected to make Charleston the major cultural center of the Southeast."[142]

Even though many community leaders were excited for the opportunities of a popular arts festival, the local citizens remained cautiously optimistic for fear of streets congested with tourists. While the crowds didn't necessarily flock to Charleston right away, the locals quickly embraced the festival's offerings. Growing larger every year, the festival provided a global spotlight on Charleston, eventually drawing an eclectic crowd of tourists and performers who would seek out opportunities for culinary adventures.

Adding to this, the mini-bottle law was finally enacted in 1973, which allowed restaurants to sell liquor drinks again. Bill Snipes, owner of The Colony House, was one of those local restaurateurs who became instrumental in helping pass this, making frequent trips to Columbia to state the case for change. Bars were a major source of income for restaurants, and once the law was passed, it offered another opportunity for increased profits and growth.

Restaurants like Marianne also began staying open late, which started to develop the previously nonexistent food-and-beverage scene in the city. Other high-quality restaurants, such as The Wine Cellar and Philippe Million, started to pop up as well, showcasing French cuisine as the new standard of fine dining in Charleston. Residents could finally find quality meals in their own city, and culinary styles began to expand from there.

A 1980 article in the local paper detailed the sharp increase in restaurants, stating that between 1972 and 1980 in Charleston County, "businesses that sell food for a profit have seen a 153.3 percent increase in gross sales."[143] But this growth was still met with a fair amount of concern. An explosion of restaurant choices with a limited number of customers meant everyone received smaller slices of the pie. Increased competition from chain and fast-food restaurants, along with rising operating costs of small businesses, left some feeling weary about the future.

However, for the most part, the growth was viewed with an optimistic eye. When interviewed about the restaurant boom in 1980, Mayor Riley reiterated the importance of restaurants to a city's economic health. "A good city—a city with excitement and spirit—needs a number of good restaurants," he said. When questioned if it was possible to have too many restaurants downtown, he added, "I don't think so. As the city's revitalization continues, we'll have more and more restaurant customers. Plus, free enterprise will regulate the number of restaurants. A new establishment will have to be better than existing ones, or it won't make it. Existing ones will have to be

Bill Snipes behind the bar at The Colony House on Vendue Range. He was one of many restaurant owners to push for the "mini-bottle" law. *From Ginny Snipes.*

able to withstand the competition." He then added, "When I was growing up, you could count the number of good restaurants on one hand. Now, it's hard to keep up with them. They're important to the city, in tax base and jobs for the people of the city."[144]

The increase in restaurants also brought more suppliers to the area, as many restaurateurs initially had a difficult time securing quality ingredients. One chef and restaurateur remembers having to deal with a seafood vendor who left quite a bit to be desired in terms of quality, but without any other choices in the city, he couldn't be too picky. Fortunately, when more restaurants began requiring supplies, more wholesalers started shipping to the area and allowed for a wider variety of offerings.

The opening of Johnson and Wales culinary school in 1984 helped attract those interested in culinary careers, while the opening of the Omni Hotel in 1986 brought visitors to the often-neglected market area. These dramatic changes in the city allowed for changes in the restaurant scene as well, bonding together a small group of talented restaurant owners. Technically

The empty lot across from The Colony House has changed significantly over the years. It is now home to Joe Riley Waterfront Park. *From Celia Cerasoli.*

competitors, they gathered at meetings for the Charleston Restaurant Association, dined at each other's restaurants and supported one another in their ventures. Nearly every owner I spoke with from this time period mentioned the close-knit restaurant community—a feat of connectedness that would be nearly impossible these days simply due to the volume of restaurants in town.

This tremendous growth and change continued until September 1989, when Hurricane Hugo struck the South Carolina coast. The storm had reached a monstrous category five status as it headed toward the Caribbean. It weakened but then restrengthened to a category four when it finally made landfall just a few miles north of Charleston. The storm caused numerous power outages, washed boats ashore in piles and destroyed homes and businesses.

The damage brought the city together in an attempt to rebuild, but the repairs and renovations from Hugo's devastation would take decades to fully complete. In this trying time, Charleston's restaurants continued to play an important part in the rebuilding process. Gaulart & Maliclet (also known as Fast and French), a local favorite for thirty-five years, set a prime example when it created a beacon of hope in a time of loss. The café opened just two days after the storm, without power or water, and did its part to bring back a sense of community through some of Charleston's best offerings: food and hospitality.

ROBERT'S OF CHARLESTON

Charleston should be thankful that when Robert Dickson narrowed down his career choices between a banker and a cook, he chose the latter. After attending the Culinary Institute of America, traveling in France and even studying with Julia Child, Dickson had many incredible opportunities to hone his culinary talents. He got to work in various restaurants around the United States before settling down on Hilton Head Island to become a part owner of the Hofbräuhaus restaurant in 1973. However, after the business partnership didn't work out, Dickson decided to take a step back from the restaurant scene. A far departure from his usual day to day in the kitchen, he decided it was time to focus on his other passion: singing. Just as he had invested time in developing his culinary skills, Dickson studied music at Kent State University and fostered his natural talent.

A few years later, in 1976, Dickson ran into his former boss, Franz Meier, who needed some help at The Colony House. Dickson came to Charleston to help with the restaurant's transition to new ownership but told Meier he wouldn't be able to stay for long. He knew he wanted to work for himself and was already planning something of his own. After three months at The Colony House, Dickson left to open Robert's of Charleston—a business that would combine his passions of cooking and singing.

The 530 square feet of storefront space in the Rainbow Market was never intended to be a restaurant. Surrounded by specialty shops, the other owners weren't necessarily excited about the idea of a restaurant in their midst. "They thought of rats and flies and bad smells," Robert said of the initial reception to his restaurant's home.[145] The landlord was also skeptical of Robert's vision, wondering how anyone could possibly put an entire restaurant in such a small space. But the rent was affordable for the location and that was an appealing feature for a brand-new investment.

Dickson was able to transform the storefront into a fine dining haven by completing a lot of the work himself. However, the task of collecting commercial appliances was no easy feat, and his scavenger hunt took him all the way to a discount appliance store in Canton, Ohio. On the way home in his rented truck, Dickson had to make a stop in Atlanta to pick up a stove. The large appliance just happened to be in a residential home with a fairly precarious flight of stairs. They managed to shimmy the stove down to the all-too-far-away truck with a little ingenuity and some plywood on the stairs. The project of building a restaurant seemed to be a true labor of love.

With the kitchen finally in place, Dickson mounted a piano on a platform and still managed to fit a cozy twenty-eight seats in the dining room. The concept was unique: Robert would be cooking, performing songs and serving the guests a multicourse meal. When Robert's of Charleston officially opened on July 1, 1976, Dickson and his wife, Pam, started with a lunch service to get a feel for the routine but quickly added a popular eight o'clock dinner service. The small space was perfect for the warm ambiance Dickson wanted to create, and guests left feeling like new friends after attending the three-hour dinner service.

The restaurant's concept took off. In fact, local newspapers printed two articles about Robert's of Charleston within a few days in 1977, and the restaurant was booked for weeks at a time. The little shops surrounding the restaurant were even a bit annoyed at the lines stemming from Robert's popularity, though it was bringing quite a few people to the Rainbow Market.

Those lucky guests who scored reservations were in for a one-of-a-kind experience. The setup might have been overwhelming to the fine dining novice, with place settings of ten different pieces of cutlery and three different glasses. But the simple decor and charm of the staff is what made Robert's feel like home. When the piano struck a chord, the lights dimmed, the waiters took their cue to retreat to their respective corners and out would come Robert Dickson, shining in the spotlight. The next course would be displayed high in the air as he belted out his signature "Food, Glorious Food" in a rich baritone. Passing along each table, he would offer a glimpse of the dish before stopping to slice up individual servings—never missing a beat in the process. It was an impressive feat to simultaneously wear the hats of an opera singer and chef.

While they made the process look effortless, Dickson and his wife worked constantly in those beginning months. When one of the only local laundry services returned wrinkled tablecloths, they literally took the dirty laundry home with them. He remembers loading the tablecloths and napkins into the back of their station wagon and driving down to the Battery after a long, successful evening. Just in the midst of saying, "Wasn't that a good night," a warm summer breeze would carry a whiff of those dirty linens from the back seat—perhaps a slightly less appealing smell of success.

 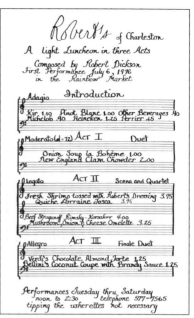

Left: Robert's of Charleston's first lunch menu with calligraphy done by Robert's wife, Pam. *From Robert Dickson.*

Right: A musical themed menu from Robert's of Charleston. *From Robert Dickson.*

There were a few other kinks to work though, which is typical of any new business. Before they invested in a copy machine, Pam Dickson would create the calligraphy on the menus by hand every day for each of the tables, even taking a class to perfect her skills. It also took time to get the air conditioning correct in the space, and they dealt with a leaky window unit for a while. The food, however, was spot on from the get-go.

The six-course fixed menu was carefully set up before the meal, which meant that every person got the same high level of service. Though a few locals requested some family dishes, Robert's stuck with Dickson's own home cooking. A testament to his skill, most people were willing to sit down and try whatever he placed in front of them—all ending with rave reviews. Dining to the sound of songs from *Camelot*, *My Fair Lady*, *Fiddler on the Roof* and *Oliver*, as well as operatic arias, many described their experience at Robert's as the highlight of their visit to Charleston.

Never shy about sharing the details of his recipes, Dickson even published several cookbooks. A testament to his skill in the kitchen, he knew that people at home wouldn't necessarily be able to re-create the magic of dining in his restaurant. As he explained in an interview in 1977, "It just won't be the same, like artwork or singing, only the person who wrote the song knows exactly how it is supposed to be."[146] He recalled that people had some success re-creating his Chateaubriand, but most other recipes were too intricate to try to re0create. This is evident in his cookbook *Robert's Dinner for Six*, where a novice such as myself became overwhelmed simply by the table setting list that included "at least nine pieces of china for each guest, five forks, two spoons and two knives, two wine glasses, candles, serving dishes, sauce boat, serving spoons and platters"—a simple reminder of why it's almost always worth going out to eat.[147]

In 1980, Frank Jarrell wrote about his experience at the restaurant, calling his meal of spinach and mushroom roulade, scallop mousse with lobster sauce and the signature Chateaubriand "one of the best meals we've ever had."[148] Crowds were in love with Robert's of Charleston, and the enthusiasm of the city was infectious. In fact, the unique and captivated audience at Robert's was such a joy to experience that his piano player once said, "My husband says I would come and play here, even if they didn't pay me."[149]

By 1988, Robert's was enjoying almost $1 million in sales, and the restaurant moved into the Planters Inn. At the height of the business's popularity, even Paul Newman couldn't get a reservation. When he called to get seats one day, the hostess had to inform him that they were completely booked. Upon hearing of Newman's request to dine at his restaurant, Dickson sprang into action, bringing a set of chairs from home to add the necessary two spots. However, when he casually mentioned that a friend of his had given up his seats to make room, Paul Newman said he couldn't possibly force such an inconvenience. Robert's was also the city's first Four Diamond restaurant— an honor it received four times—and Dickson appeared in countless papers, magazines and local television programs. He even sold cassette tapes of his singing for Christmas stocking stuffers. His celebrity garnered a lot of attention, and some guests would even attempt to stop him for a starstruck chat in the middle of a dinner service.

While Robert's popularity skyrocketed in the late '80s, the growth wasn't without its own unique challenges. Dickson even found himself double-booked one night, but the show still went on. Forced to run between his restaurant and Robert's Other Place around the corner, Dickson hired an additional pianist and, in some feat of superhero-level multitasking, performed two shows at once. Business reached its peak right before Hurricane Hugo in 1989, when Robert was seating more than one hundred people per night. They had only been in their new home at the Planters

A JOURNAL OF FINE COOKING

by

ROBERT DICKSON

Robert Dickson has published several cookbooks. *A Journal of Fine Cooking* features his restaurant at the Planters Inn. *From Robert Dickson.*

Inn for a year when the storm hit. While Robert's never again reached the success of what it was before the storm, the term "Charleston institution" was already well earned. In May 1994, when a lease couldn't be agreed on with the inn's new owner, Robert's of Charleston closed.

Dickson toyed around with what to do next. He later recalled, "I didn't have a plan in 1994 when I closed, and that was a disaster."[150] Burned on the idea of having a landlord, he considered opening a restaurant in Charlotte or perhaps something where he could be a little less involved. At that point, he had been the owner, the chef and the entertainment every night. Taking time off can be difficult when you're the star of the show, but Robert wouldn't stop completely. Later that year, he took up a short residency at Restaurant Million before taking the next few years off. During that time, he became a tour guide in Italy and took a few private catering gigs.

After a four-year hiatus, Dickson was ready to come back. He found a new location on East Bay Street that could seat forty people. The place was an opportunity to create a small, intimate experience again after the growth of his previous restaurant space. Robert and Pam continued to run the restaurant with minimal staff to keep prices as low as possible, but the restaurant was still considered a special occasion destination with its multicourse meals. When asked about his return in 1998, Robert said, "I never really thought I'd do it again."[151] This was especially true with the exponential increase in the cost of opening a business in the late '90s versus the '70s, and the idea that he'd be back on his feet all day long. He stated the most difficult part of coming back "was finding the right location for the right price."[152] He was lucky leasing a space on the well-traveled East Bay Street that once was home to an old café. Since it was already set up as a restaurant, it required much less outfitting.

Robert's daughter, MariElana, and her husband, Joe, helped continue the legacy at his restaurant's East Bay Street location. *From Robert Dickson.*

The revamped Robert's faced its own unique challenges over the years. In 2001, Cypress opened across the street and offered a similar menu, and tourism business in Charleston varied in the early 2000s. Dickson still enjoyed his return to glory as chef and entertainer, but in 2006, he was ready to close up shop. That was, until his daughter, MariElena Reya, and her husband, Joe Reya, came up from Florida to work with him.

While many children of restaurant owners shy away from the business, Robert's daughter had the opposite experience. In an interview with the author, she stated, "I never had the stereotypical aversion to the restaurant industry despite being raised in it." She saw the benefits of owning your own business, and her husband encouraged the idea of opening something of their own. MariElena had attended the Culinary Institute of America, her father's alma mater, and had met her eventual husband there.

MariElena and Joe continued the traditions of Robert's, serving up favorites like corn pancakes with dumplings, spinach quiche and chocolate chestnut torte, until Robert's official retirement in 2010. When asked if they would continue the business, Joe stated, "We couldn't even imagine running it without Robert."[153] Instead, they took the opportunity to create something brand new in the space on East Bay. Their cocktail spot, The Gin Joint, opened a few months after Robert's retirement.

A business project that focused mostly on the beverage scene was ideally less time consuming for the busy, young family. It was good timing on their part, as the attention on craft cocktails in Charleston was just starting to take off with the free-pour liquor law taking over the formerly restrictive mini bottles. Even though The Gin Joint was a complete transformation from Robert's concept, people still assumed that he owned it. This was a reputation they didn't mind having as a brand-new establishment. MariElena explained, "My dad's reputation in town got us so much further than we could have on our own, so we welcomed people thinking that."

They even held a few Robert's of Charleston throwback dinners in the space, which were incredibly popular and a testament to Robert's long-lasting popularity. MariElena spoke of her dad's legacy, stating "Robert's customers were so dedicated and that is a testament to my dad always being there at night, speaking to each guest."

The Gin Joint is still on East Bay but is no longer a part of the Robert's family. MariElena and Joe sold the spot in 2017 to focus on a line of handcrafted cocktail mixers. They now own Bittermilk, Tippleman's and Barcoop Bevy and have a production facility in North Charleston. This set up, just a bit removed from the restaurant scene, is a good fit for the Reya family. When asked if they might consider owning a restaurant again, MariElena said she'd consider it when their kids were a bit older—a hopeful thought for those who got to experience their talents.

Robert Dickson guesses he served between 120,000 and 150,000 people during his time as chef and stated, "I will miss my customers. I will miss my culinary children," in an interview about his retirement.[154] At that time, he also spoke of the energy required to run a business, especially with the passion he demonstrated—he only missed a few days in his entire career. No one has ever tried to imitate what he created, perhaps because it just can't be done. Described as a "natural born entertainer," a "Charleston institution," "legendary" and "unquestionably one of the best chefs in town," Robert Dickson certainly earned the legacy of Charleston's Singing Chef.[155]

MARIANNE

Marianne is the symbol of the French Republic, representing freedom and democracy. In Charleston, it represented one of our finest French restaurants. Serge Claire first opened Marianne in 1977 at 219 Meeting Street and was described in a 1977 *Post and Courier* feature as "volatile, exuberant, knowledgeable and mischievous."[156] If a customer ordered a steak very well done, he'd be so inclined to serve them a black leather boot on a silver tray.

An experienced chef and restaurateur, Claire, like so many before and after him, landed in Charleston after someone mentioned he should visit. In what should be our city motto, he said, "I came. I looked. I stayed."[157] His menu's most lavish dishes included the Poivre Vert, Chateaubriand for two and rack of lamb. However, one of the restaurant's most unique offering was a late-night breakfast from 10:00 p.m. to 2:00 a.m., which was a welcome addition to Charleston's lackluster nightlife scene. These late-night breakfasts were especially popular after Spoleto Festival events, as steak tartare might just be one of the best hangover cures. Plus, with European influence on the rise in Charleston, more locals were up for trying French cuisine. Claire reported to the local paper in 1982, "They ask me, 'What is French food?' I say, well, maybe American food with a little more flavor. But I have to be careful how I describe it."[158]

In June 1982, Claire was involved in a bit of a showdown with none other than Charleston mayor Joseph P. Riley Jr. In the quest to build the Charleston Center hotel and retail complex—a major factor in the revitalization of King Street—the city needed to acquire the restaurant at 219 Meeting Street. This wasn't the end for Claire, as he was already building a larger restaurant farther up the street, but he needed to keep the current space until the new one was ready.

The condemnation proceedings placed a $185,000 price tag on his building, but while Claire felt it was worth more, the city felt it was worth much less. This negotiation was important for the business owner, since the cost of his new restaurant was close to $750,000.[159] He couldn't afford to lose revenue by closing one business before the new one was ready, and the jobs of thirty-five people were on the line if they had to find work elsewhere before the new location opened. Luckily, the downtime between restaurant moves was minimal, as Marianne announced closure due to condemnation on October 30, 1982, and opened in the new space at 235 Meeting on November 8. The sixteen-thousand-square-foot building on

A Touch of France

MARIANNE

DINNER 6 - 10:30
AFTER SHOW SUPPER
11:00 P.M., - 1:30 A.M.

235 Meeting St., Charleston, SC
For reservations, phone 722-7196
Intimate Dining or Festive Private Parties

Above: Marianne's original location at 219 Meeting Street in the 1970s. *From Historic Charleston Foundation Archives.*

Left: A Marianne advertisement from 1984 promoted the restaurant's new location. *From* On The Towne *vol. 3, 1984.*

the corner of Meeting and Hasell Streets was where Claire would operate for another thirteen years.

When health problems arose, Claire decided to take a break from the strain of the restaurant business, and Marianne served its last meal on New Year's Eve in 1995. For a cool $1.3 million, the building changed hands to become a Sticky Fingers barbecue restaurant, as it remains today.[160] In the local paper on January 8, 1996, the new owners of Sticky Fingers ran an advertisement thanking Serge Claire and wishing him well in retirement. They also included a promise to provide high-quality food and service, as was expected in that particular location, but they made sure to remind the public that they were a completely different style of restaurant.[161] The restaurant's change was a powerful example of the transfer of trust required to take over an established local favorite.

THE GOURMETISSERIE

The old warehouses positioned on the corner of South Market and Church Streets were originally slated to become a high-rise condominium in the 1970s. That was until the Save Charleston Foundation stepped in to sell the property to the Save Charleston Partnership for restoration. Harold Adler was the architect of the $4 million development known as Market Square, complete with 12,500 square feet of food court space known as the Gourmetisserie.[162] Opened in 1977, Adler commented that he wanted it to be a spot for locals and tourists alike, seeking out owner-operated stores over franchises.

Adler's idea was incredibly successful and brought in people from all walks of life with a variety of food to choose from. In 1977, the restaurants included Old Athens, Low Country Kitchen, Deli Den, Theo's Pizza, Hot Diggity Dog, Cousin's Fried Chicken, Bessinger's Barbecue, Beef n' Bun, Crepes and Cakes, Soups and Salads, the Frozen Yogurt Place, Sylvester's Seafood and Puffy Egg. Each storefront lined the open space of tables and chairs that were constantly transforming with the various groups of visitors.

Local business owners would eat at the Gourmetisserie once, twice or every single day of the week. The selection was vast, and the prices were reasonable, with service fast enough for a quick lunch break. One news feature from 1977 described the scene: "It's a melting pot of people from Charleston—businessmen from Broad Street and secretaries from uptown—

and people from other parts of the world."[163] Local Jeannette Weldon called the setting "long overdue," while a local tour guide, Jane Thornhill, commented that she was happy to see "the city come back from derelict and horror to charm and beauty."[164]

Even in the restaurant guides, the Gourmetisserie flaunted its diverse choices and low price points: "Head for the Gourmetisserie when you're looking for an extraordinary treat at ordinary prices."[165] While the local tour books stated, "Enter the world of culinary delights featuring a unique array of hand prepared international foods."[166]

Local musicians frequently provided evening entertainment, and the space was also a venue to host Spoleto Festival events. Although it was a true part of the community, the Gourmetisserie was gone by the turn of the century. With continued growth in Charleston on the horizon, Batson Hewitt and Jay Keenan had big plans to change the block into a new hotel. The Board of Zoning Appeals had even approved a special exception for the fifty-room venture.[167] While we tend to have different reactions today, at the time, residents appeared to be supportive of the changes, welcoming what would soon become the French Quarter Inn.

With the opening of a food court setup, the Workshop, on North Morrison Street, people can't help but continue to draw comparisons to the old standard and the fond remembrance for the ability to eat reasonably priced food on a daily basis.

SAN MIGUEL'S

Not far from the Gourmetisserie stood San Miguel's. The first mention of this restaurant is a review by critic Frank Jarrell in February 1980.[168] Located in the back of Market Square, behind the Market Street Plaza, this restaurant offered a touch of much-needed variety to the restaurant scene in Charleston at the time.

The decor hinted at the menu's flair, with sombreros and images of bull fights on the wall, but it didn't necessarily scream the message. Of course, there was the quintessential basket of corn chips and entrées served with rice and beans, but customers could also find chili rellenos, huge burritos and huevos rancheros. Those feeling brave could order the intimidating Montezuma's Revenge, or simply stick with the popular crab meat enchiladas, which were a mixture of crab meat, sour cream, spices and a touch more sour cream.

A regular fixture at the Taste of Charleston, San Miguel's would often serve up crab meat enchiladas and chili con queso. But back at the restaurant, the focus was on the good food and a popular happy hour. Young professionals had adopted the restaurant as their hangout, and you'd often see these executives and medical students hanging out on the patio. In fact, one article from the summer of 1988 called San Miguel's "a popular happy hour hangout for younger yuppies."[169]

Bob Olin, owner of San Miguel's and a veteran of the restaurant business, could also claim a little credit in the rise of singer Edwin McCain. His first gigs were right on Market Street in the late '80s, and noticing a true talent, Olin passed along the singer's demo tape.[170] McCain eventually landed a record deal, and his song "I'll Be" has easily been stuck in your head since the late '90s. Unfortunately, the restaurant suffered the same fate as the Gourmetisserie and was eventually torn down in the late '90s to make way for the French Quarter Inn.

GARIBALDI'S

John Sutcliffe opened Garibaldi's in 1977 and named it after an Italian patriot from the 1800s who fought to unite his country. The location was a red brick building from 1830, right in the heart of the City Market and originally sat a cozy forty-two people.

Even though the market area is often associated with tourism, Garibaldi's owner estimated that 75 percent of the business was return customers, meaning he was able to capture the local crowd.[171] The reviews over the years were largely positive. While the restaurant was loud and a bit cramped at times, it was still considered cozy and casual. The quality of the food didn't go down with the influx of tourists—a welcome scene as the market became more popular.

The menu was focused on Northern Italian cuisine, which uses a fair amount of cream and butter. While the waiter might have recited an impressively long list of specials, guests couldn't go wrong with some of the standbys at Garibaldi's, including the pimento and anchovy appetizer or garlic bread which, of course, might need to be refilled a few times. Popular entrées of seafood, veal and lamb were served with a side of spaghetti, but it was the crispy flounder that stood out as a Garibaldi's highlight. The dish was created by Chef Dan Kim and featured a whole fried flounder with an apricot shallot glaze. This restaurant became a place where customers could linger for a moment with a good glass of wine or sip on an espresso from one of the city's first restaurants to acquire such a foreign machine.

The end came in 2010 when the lease on the building expired, coupled with the many changes in the availability of parking and local traffic that occurred on Market Street. The owners were experienced restaurateurs who also owned Anson Restaurant on Anson Street and the Olde Pink House in Savannah. The group had other properties in the city as well, so it was difficult to justify renting a space when they had other vacant areas. The plan was to move Garibaldi's into one of those renovated spaces, but it never came to fruition. The space was later leased by the same group that owns 82 Queen, and they opened Lowcountry Bistro that lasted until 2018, when it was converted into the fourth location for the popular barbecue joint Swig and Swine. However, the famous crispy flounder dish can still be found on the menu at Anson Restaurant.

A.W. SHUCKS

The Condon family name has been associated with shopping and eating establishments in Charleston for decades. Tommy and Edward "Skipper" Condon just happened to create their own restaurant empire back in the days when tourism wasn't so popular, especially in the market area, where they later dominated. Tommy was many things before venturing into the restaurant industry, including a medic in Vietnam, a fireman, funeral director and bar manager, while Skipper had previously worked for the family's well-known Condon's Department Store.[172] Their food and beverage partnership began in 1981 on the USS *Yorktown*, where they ran concessions. Two years later, they were able to use their savings to purchase A.W. Shucks Seafood Warehouse Restaurant and Raw Bar and another building, which would later become an Irish pub called Tommy Condon's.

Since they had familiar names within the community, Tommy and Skipper put their feet to work canvasing the town to spread the word about their restaurants. They brought in whatever business they could find. Beginning the long-standing tradition of promotions and collaborative deals with tour guides, they offered great deals to get people in the door.

The menu grew over the years and was filled with traditional Lowcountry dishes as well as impressive feats, such as shrimp stuffed with deviled crab, wrapped in bacon and deep fried. Since they were offering relatively inexpensive seafood in a tourist hotspot, the restaurant came to be quite popular. In fact, many other establishments in the area would orient potential customers to their location by way of their restaurant, advertising they were "next door to A.W. Shucks" or "across the street from A.W. Shucks," which is an impressive feat of rootedness.

Skipper and Tommy Condon sold the business to John Keener of Charleston Crab House in 2015, with the idea of focusing on their remaining businesses in town: Bocci's and Tommy Condon's, as well as two successful pubs in Virginia. Keener ran the restaurant for a year to get a proper feel for the place before officially closing it down in 2016 to renovate and open under a new concept called the Oyster House on Market.

BOCCI'S

When Tommy and Skipper opened Bocci's in 1990, they had a naming competition within the company. Bocci's was catchy and easy to remember, and it was a solid reference to the Italian cuisine they offered. However, when the restaurant on Church Street joined Condon's group of restaurants, they didn't shout it from the rooftops. "We downplayed our ownership. Between Tommy Condon's and Shucks, Charleston people thought all we knew were fried shrimp, cold beer and hamburgers," Skipper Condon told the local paper in 2000.[173]

The restaurant's building dates back to 1867 and was built by the Molony family to replace a set of smaller buildings that were destroyed in the Great Fire of 1861 that swept across the peninsula. The first floor was originally a grocery storefront, and family living space was available above. A saloon also operated on the premises, but with the dispensary laws restricting the sale of liquor in the 1890s, the official title was removed from the location. However, that didn't mean it stopped operating—especially in Charleston where many of these liquor laws were blatantly ignored—it just meant it was likely one of the many blind tiger locations in town. Some have even credited this location as the city's first Irish pub, considering the Molony family's heritage.[174]

The Molony property was first outfitted for a restaurant in the '70s with credit to the increase in tourist activity in the nearby City Market. Unfortunately, the building was one of the many damaged by Hurricane

Bocci's was once home to a speakeasy and may be destined to become another hotel. *From the author.*

Hugo in 1989. At that point, the Condon brothers took over to renovate and open Bocci's. An excellent location just a block from Market Street, the comfortable Italian restaurant had terra-cotta tiled floors, dark wooden furniture and subtle Italian touches like stucco walls with stenciled details. Pasta, meat and seafood dishes were the focus of the restaurant's menu.

The restaurant closed in 2015, not too long after the Condon brothers sold A.W. Shucks to John Keener. The Board of Architectural Review, which oversees development and preservation of old structures in the historic district, approved plans to create a new hotel on the site in 2016.

NORM'S

Norm's wasn't run down, it was weathered with love from college students, MUSC employees and locals in the Harleston Village. Opened in 1979, the iconic corner building stood on Smith and Calhoun in all of its primary color glory. It had even survived a devastating fire only nine years into its tenure but recovered to continue on for decades.

Norm's was a place for cheap pitchers of beer, a game of pool or a quick but filling lunch. The famous mascot, a cartoon chef with an impressive mustache, was always waiting to greet the customer's order. Of the many items to choose from, guests might grab a meatball and cheese sub with house-made marinara on their lunch break, a huge calzone capable of inducing a food coma right before an afternoon class or maybe a few chicken wings to cap off a night out.

Feeling the effects of burnout, Norm Hanf retired for a bit after twenty years in the business. The break gave Traye Collins and Richard Corn the opportunity to step in and keep things running, and they were careful not to change too much in the process. There were rumors that the business might close in 2010, which had the city buzzing, but Norm and his family stepped back into ownership to the delight of all Charlestonians. Eventually, after thirty-seven years, the restaurant closed for good.

Soon after, Dave Uecke took over the reins in the space, with some help from local pizza gurus Ben and Nick D'Allesandro of D'Allesandro's Pizza. At first, they attempted to keep things running under the same name, but subtle changes, including the shape of the pizza, were noticed by the public. The new owners acknowledged the difficulties of taking over an established restaurant that had been open for more than thirty years, especially when Norm's menu had grown significantly over time and loyal customers wanted to make sure they could still get the variety they wanted.

They eventually acknowledged the switch of ownership when they changed the name of the restaurant to Smith Street Pizza, but they still tried to stick with the early 2000s vibe that Norm's used to have.[175] However, the closure three months later may have been a sign of a bit too much change at once, as people were still holding the menu in comparison to Norm's. The closure of Smith Street Pizza allowed Brown Dog Deli to step in and assume the space as their business's second location. Owners Wes Denney and Brent Petterson made a few drastic changes to the restaurant, and while their concept was a complete departure from the legend of the past, they kept Norm's Italian sub on the menu. Unfortunately, history repeated itself and Brown Dog Deli announced the closure of the Calhoun Street location in May 2019. The space awaits its next concept.

EAST BAY TRADING COMPANY

Built in 1880, the Wagener-Ohlandt building conveys a different time period in Charleston. It began as the home of F.W. Wagener and Company, a business that dealt in many of the popular trades of the nineteenth century, including cotton, fertilizer and grocery offerings. F.W. Wagener also happened to be president of the Exposition Company and helped bring the South Carolina Inter-state and West Indian Exposition to town in 1901.

The massive building consumes the corner of East Bay and Queen Streets with three stories of arched brick windows. Tour guides often suggest the building's third floor is haunted by the ghost of a ruined businessman, complete with mysterious cold breezes and misplaced objects. While the facts of these stories are difficult to confirm, it remains a subject of ghost tours and Charleston lore.

East Bay Trading Company was the first restaurant to make use of the Wagener-Ohlandt building in 1980. Taking up eighteen thousand square feet of the three-story building, it's easy to understand why the restaurant renovations were more than $1 million.[176] The transformation from warehouse to restaurant hot spot was one of those key moments for the city's revitalization, according to Mayor Riley, who was in attendance at the opening ceremonies.

The decor of the restaurant was less than subtle and included a San Francisco cable car, high-wheel bicycles and a giant phone booth. Large planters hung from the ceiling attempted to fill in the open space of the atrium. The restaurant oozed atmosphere and managed to capture the beauty of the building without feeling too much like the old warehouse it once was.

East Bay Trading Company opened to quite a bit of anticipation and dealt with large crowds right from its beginning. The hustle and bustle seemed to rely mostly on a tourist crowd, but the nightlife scene was luckily vibrant in the surrounding area. When the restaurant closed in

Left: F.W. Wagener was president of the Exposition Company and helped bring the event to town. *From Official Guide: South Carolina Inter-State and West Indian Exposition, 1901.*

Below: The Wagener-Ohlandt building has undergone major renovations. *From the author.*

1995, it didn't remain empty for long. Southend Brewery took over and established the spot as a restaurant and brewery with the perfect event space for wedding receptions.

When the building was purchased by Lagunitas Brewing in 2016, the community had mixed reactions. While it was difficult to let go of a local business, the size and potential needs of the historic building were possibly better suited for the deep pockets of a large company. Unfortunately, the building proved to require more work than anyone was anticipating. A year after gaining the space, Lagunitas had to abruptly close when the structure needed costly and immediate repair. Scaffolding was even placed around the building to protect pedestrians from potential falling bricks.

While a building abruptly shifting from hot spot to pedestrian hazard seems like a fairly shocking problem, it's not that uncommon in a city like Charleston. Restaurants operating in historic buildings face potentially monumental costs of repairs or upkeep every day. The same situation happened to Nick's Original BBQ on King Street in 2017, when it had to abruptly shutter due to the state of the building, which required scaffolding, steel beam supports and redirected pedestrian traffic.

PHILIPPE MILLION

Philippe Million enjoyed great success as a hotelier and restaurateur in France. In fact, his restaurant in the French Alps was awarded an impressive two Michelin stars. Chi Xuan Diep, a Charlestonian who frequented this location in France, managed to convince Million that Charleston might be the perfect U.S. destination to host a classic French restaurant.

Million settled down at 2 Unity Alley, a building that dates back to 1767 and was turned into a tavern by Edward McCrady in 1778. George Washington even dined at this location during his southern tour in 1791. It served as a place to eat and drink until the early 1900s, when it was used as a warehouse and eventually became another abandoned building. Million and his business partners, Chi Xuan Dipe and Roger Menard, opened the restaurant as Philippe Million Tavern Historique in 1983.

Their chef was José de Anacleto, a young, talented chef who was born in Portugal and moved to France at age thirteen. He graduated from the culinary school Thonon-Les Bains in Haute Savoie, France, and was a protégé of Philippe Million, though de Anacleto described Million like a father figure and "more than a mentor."[177] He also spent considerable time working in French restaurants adorned with two and three Michelin stars.

The 1983 menu originally had two lists. The Menu Gourmand offered seven courses for thirty dollars, and the Menu Degustation offered nine courses for forty dollars. The first two years were challenging as the general public might not have known what to expect from one of the city's first authentic and classic French restaurants. Million emphasized the fact that the focus was quality, not quantity. "The cuisine is designed not to stuff but to satisfy," he stated in a 1983 interview.[178] He was dismissive of the idea that guests might be a little off put by the amount of food received for the price.

However, in a 1983 review by Frank Jarrell, this seemed to be exactly the case. Jarrell was unimpressed by the restaurant's portion sizes and described receiving "about two tablespoons of soup in the bottom of a cup. It tasted like somewhat thinned, condensed milk that had been flavored with the essence of shrimp."[179] He also described perfectly cooked but bland fish and a garnish more satisfying than the main dish itself. "French cuisine is noted for serving numerous small courses. That's fine, but it's reasonable to expect each of those tidbits to be a delight. This is not so the evening we were at Philippe Million."[180]

Philippe *Million*

NOUVELLE CUISINE
Your choice of á la carte
and prix fixe menus.
Dinner 6:30 - 11 pm
Reservations required: 577-7472
Two Unity Alley (off East Bay St. one block north of Broad St.)
★ ★ ★ *"Everybody ought to eat here once in this life*
to experience the finest food possible."

Philippe Million advertisement from 1984. *From* On The Towne *vol. 3, 1984.*

Although he later clarified in a review that "it wasn't that the food was bad. It's just that there wasn't enough of it. In fact, I went to a fast-food place on the way home."[181] Jarrell's review was met with disagreement from the general public. One customer commented they were "moved to contact you [Jarrell] because I strongly disagree with your assessment of this delightful new restaurant."[182] Additional menus and positive customer comments were sent along for review in a response from Ray Easler and Philippe Million. They suggested the menus would assist Jarrell "if he is ever allowed to write about French cuisine again….After all, quality is an acquired taste, but we hope that it's not too late for Mr. Jarrell to get it."[183]

The crew at Philippe Million stuck to their guns, and two years after opening, they earned the Relais Gourmand rating from Relais et Châteaux, which is a French fine dining and hotel guide. They also earned a more positive review from the local paper in 1985. The details made the service memorable this time around, as the review described the attentive ashtray service and the waiters lifting domes off the entrées with a collective, "Voilà!" Perhaps ending with a slightly different perspective of the small plate experience, writer Christine W. Randall described her meal as "a lighter approach to gourmet dining."[184] Thankfully, she didn't mention stopping for fast food afterward.

In 1988, Chef José de Anacleto partnered with a financial backer named William J. Gilliam to buy out the restaurant and the Long Room club upstairs. This partner allowed the chef to focus on the food and not have to worry so much about the money. Restaurant Million, as it was known then, didn't change too much. However, at that time, de Anacleto had "become more accustomed to American tastes and adjusted portions accordingly."[185]

This adjustment earned a more positive review from Jarrell, who was happy with his meal featuring smoked salmon with paprika sauce, scallops on scrambled eggs with green peppercorns, filet mignon and lamb dishes. The restaurant had solidly established its reputation for fine dining, and Jarrell recommended it for a special occasion as long as guests didn't mind paying for the service.[186] The *Chicago Tribune* mentioned the restaurant in 1991 and reminded potential guests to "budget at least two hours and $200"[187] for the experience, while restaurateur Dick Elliott said, "It was French to the nth degree and Charleston's most upscale restaurant."[188]

Just as the future was looking incredibly bright for Restaurant Million, Hurricane Hugo plowed through the city. The restaurant lost thousands of bottles of wine and suffered significant structural damage, so the owners took the opportunity to renovate the building during the repair process.

Along with structural changes, they restored the building's original stairway back to the way it was in 1778 and added an additional dining room on the third floor. They also began to steer the menu toward traditional haute cuisine to mirror what was happening in Europe. "Things are a little simpler, the sauces are very light," de Anacleto described in 1990.[189]

In March 1990, de Anacleto ran an advertisement to welcome patrons back to the two restaurants housed within the space. "With a new decor, a renewed spirit, and a grand menu featuring prix-fixe and à-la-carte, Restaurant Million and The Long Room Club is waiting to serve you."[190]

De Anacleto was also eager to teach, and while he started an exchange program with chefs from France, many familiar Charleston chefs studied under him as well. Brent Petterson, who has owned and operated restaurants in Charleston for more than fifteen years said, "José was the best chef I ever worked for," in an interview with the author. After all, local legend Frank Lee served as his sous chef in the 1990s, and Frank McMahon of Hank's Seafood spent time there too.

In 1993, Restaurant Million moved upstairs, serving the Long Room private club members during the day and Million diners in the evening. This opened the door for McCrady's to open downstairs. McCrady's had more of a casual feel—a contrast to the candelabras, Limoges porcelain and tapestry-lined walls of Restaurant Million. However, things turned a bit sour in 1996, when Jose's partner, Gilliam, was sued for nonpayment of loans and taxes. The building was sold in October 1996, to Tavern on the Alley—a partnership with Greenbax enterprises and de Anacleto. The group paid $1.3 million for the building.[191]

Unfortunately, the partnership didn't pan out as planned. One million dollars' worth of renovations in early 1999 gutted and expanded the restaurant. It reopened in June 1999, with Michael Kramer as the new chef at McCrady's and Tradd Newton and David LeBoutillier as general partners.[192] While Restaurant Million is now gone, this particular restaurant space continues to garner national recognition for Chef Sean Brock's involvement in McCrady's.

CELIA'S PORTA VIA

Celia Cerasoli opened her restaurant on a quiet corner of Archdale and Beaufain Streets in 1985. "I was here when there was nobody here, and

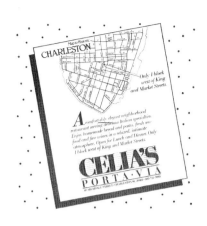

Celia's Porta Via was tucked away on Archdale and Beaufain Streets, as advertised on this promotional hand fan. *From Celia Cerasoli.*

it was pretty scary," Celia recounted in an interview in 1994.[193] She started her venture with the idea of opening a catering company, but the plan evolved when she found the perfect spot for a restaurant with an apartment above. The building was originally home to a grocery store with a little restaurant called Evangeline's, and the turnaround to Celia's Porta Via took just a few short days.

Celia was from New York, but after several visits to Charleston, she realized her heart belonged in the South. She was raised in a large Italian American family and grew up cooking, so many of her authentic recipes were passed down through her family. If anyone felt she needed more experience on her résumé, she even spent a year in Rome cultivating her skills and love of Italian cuisine. It makes sense that the menu at Celia's Porta Via was mainly Italian food, which was served up in a comfortable café setting. Delicious homemade pastas and breads were obvious stars of the show, as well as dishes that included grilled eggplant, creamy risotto and homemade mozzarella cheese. Celia even decided to keep the salad Evangeline, which consisted of tossed greens in a warm feta dressing with pine nuts, in honor of the customers who frequented the space's previous restaurant. Above all of those tasty offerings, Celia's true claim to fame was a lasagna with thirty—yes, thirty—layers.

Celia was able to buy the building she was renting after Hurricane Hugo hit in 1989. However, as the new owner, she inherited the formidable responsibility of maintaining everything. At that point, precedence had to be given to renovating the side of the building, which had started to fall off. The extensive construction project tackled the repairs, as well as the addition of a gourmet shop and pasta bar. In an act of fortunate timing, the department store Saks Fifth Avenue came to the area soon after this investment, which helped to bring an influx of people near the restaurant.

Celia's Porta Via was a gathering place for friends and family—a true local neighborhood restaurant. Families came in with their children, local students stopped in on dates and the faculty of the College of Charleston

Celia's homemade mozzarella was a favorite among guests. *From Celia Cerasoli.*

often popped in for lunch. A piano bench could be filled by anyone wishing to show off their talents, and the restaurant became known for celebrations like the "Messiah" sing-along and an Italian Carnevale dinner. Since it was such a friendly atmosphere for artists and musicians, the Spoleto Festival became one of the restaurant's busiest times of the year. If customers happened to be at Celia's late at night, they might have even been lucky enough to catch orchestra members stopping by for an encore after their official performances.

In the late '90s, the restaurant boom of Charleston caused some owners to feel the pain of increased competition with a finite number of tourists. In an interview in 1998, Celia mentioned, "The people who used to eat here once a week now eat with us once a month because there are so many other wonderful choices downtown."[194] But the biggest impact to Celia's business may have been related to Charleston's revitalization efforts. The city ended up using a parking lot next to her building as a home base for construction in the area, filling it with less-than-appealing features, such as portable toilets, large trucks and construction materials. The entire street was even torn up for quite a while, which meant that people couldn't find parking, and if they did, they would find nails in their tires from the construction debris. When

Celia's Porta Via was known for its celebrations, including Carnevale. *From Celia Cerasoli.*

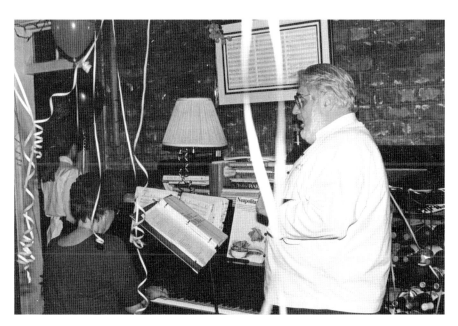

Celia's celebrations created a gathering place for locals, including the "Singing Chef," Robert Dickson. *From Celia Cerasoli.*

the city eventually decided to pave and landscape the area, it took four long months to complete.

After being closed for three months for the renovation to her own building, as well as the lack of accessible parking due to construction, it was hard for Celia to play catch-up. A small restaurant can't just double its business the next day, so recovering from a hit can be incredibly challenging. Also, since Celia had been living in the apartment above the restaurant, the business was a twenty-four-seven part of her life for years. While she loved her work, at the point when the stresses eventually outweighed the benefits of restaurant ownership, she resolved to say, "I'm done."

Although it ultimately felt like the right decision, it was easy for Celia to feel nostalgic for all of the good times and memories she had experienced in her restaurant. When she finally retired from the business in 1999, the restaurant closed with a celebration and a series of charity dinners. Her time at Celia's Porta Via was over, but Celia still had quite a lot to do. With her background in art, she worked for the Charleston Concert Association, Mepkin Abbey, and was even involved in moving an entire art collection across the Atlantic Ocean. When I brought the impressive breadth of her life experiences to her attention, Celia acknowledged, "I'm the queen of reinventing myself," a statement with which I wholeheartedly agree. In fact, Celia might just be one of my new heroes for her unwavering ability to take on any unique challenge.

Celia now often finds herself traveling between Charleston and Costa Rica with her partner, Franz Meier, who many will recall from his iconic Charleston

Local restaurateurs Celia Cerasoli and Franz Meier continue their adventures in Costa Rica. *From Celia Cerasoli.*

restaurants, The Colony House, The Wine Cellar, Carolina's and more. Meier is currently working on an impressive project to create a self-sustaining community in Costa Rica, and when I had the opportunity to speak with them for this story, they called from an actual tropical paradise, with wind chimes singing in the background. This might make us wonder why they don't sit back and enjoy retirement, but if there's one thing I've learned about successful restaurateurs in Charleston, they just can't sit still for too long.

MISTRAL

Mistral is about owners Francoise "Frenchy" and Peter Duffy as much as it is about the food they served. Francoise was from southern France and came to the United States to perfect her English so she could go back to France and teach. She met her husband, Peter, in New York, and they eventually owned a restaurant together on Long Island. They came to Charleston for a visit, and, well, we all know the rest of the story.

In 1985, the Duffys took over the restaurant space that was once known as Cabell's in the City Market. They took on the name Mistral in reference to the strong wind that blows in southern France and eventually brings in good weather. The owners felt that the sea breezes of Charleston mimicked this experience, so the name stuck. The mix of the Lowcountry and France was reflected in the menu as well.

They had onion soup, escargots en croute, crêpes, grilled meats and even put chicory on the salads. Alongside the traditional French offerings were local favorites, such as she-crab soup and blackened redfish. It was an impressive feat to introduce multiple-course meals at lunch in a city where people often just grabbed a sandwich, but as the '80s progressed, more and more French restaurants opened around them, and they had to adapt to continue to stand the test of time. The menu focused more on casual than haute cuisine, which meant offering items such as French country pâté, fried shrimp platter and coq au vin.

The interior mimicked the previous restaurant, Cabell's, but with a touch of France. There were vintage French posters on the walls and padded banquets for an added feeling of romance and intimacy. The restaurant was repeatedly described as "cozy," not pretentious or stuffy. But France wasn't the only country represented, as both French and Irish flags flew above the doorway in an homage to both of Francoise and Peter's heritages. Mistral provided a rare opportunity to celebrate both Bastille Day and St. Patrick's Day with impressive gusto.

Food aside, what stood out about Mistral was the quality of the service, the hands-on approach of the owners, the comforting atmosphere and the live music. More specifically, the jazz music. Peter and Francoise loved jazz and strongly supported local musicians. They paid someone to play in the tiny corner of the restaurant seven nights a week. It was a place where young musicians could grow their talents and play in front of a live audience, and local celebrities could do their thing. The Duffys also teamed up with JAC, a local jazz organization, and allowed it to set up a nightclub in their upstairs space, called Upstairs at Mistral, during the first two years of the Spoleto Festival. In describing the influence of jazz at Mistral, local writer Jack McCray said, "The vibe there was such that with Mistral as an example, Charleston displays the attitude of *laissez les bon temps rouler*—let the good times roll—just like its cousin, New Orleans."[195]

When the restaurant closed in the spring of 2010, the city lost a restaurant, community hang out and incubator for musical talent. Later that same year, Francoise and Peter were surprised by the JAC's Jazz Citizenship Award for their part in supporting the local jazz community. The award was a bittersweet reminder of what the community had lost in Mistral. But that wouldn't be the only loss that year, as Francoise passed away in December 2010 at the age of sixty-one. A memorial fund was established by the JAC in her honor.

CAROLINA'S

After the closure of Perdita's, local proprietors Franz Meier and Chris Weihs leased the building at 10 Exchange Street in 1987. With the success of The Colony House, The Wine Cellar and their other spaces, they certainly had a bit of experience under their belts. However, in my discussion with Meier, he said that if he had been "smart," he would have simply re-created what was successful over and over again. Instead he kept trying something different with each new restaurant he opened. Charleston is lucky he did, or else we wouldn't have seen the likes of Carolina's (or Sprouts and Krauts or Old Munich and so on).

Their goal was to create a fine dining establishment that was open for the late-night crowd. In my conversation with Celia Cerasoli and Franz Meier, Celia remembered being at a Restaurant Association meeting in Myrtle Beach when Meier first mentioned his new restaurant concept and how it would likely surprise people. While he didn't quite remember the exchange, she recalled the exact moment he revealed such an exciting idea.

To start, the exhibition kitchen of Carolina's was a novel idea at the time. The interior design was modern with a large dining room decorated in black and white that was hardly recognizable as Charleston. It could be loud, uninhibited and a lot of fun; it was a place for people to come together and simply enjoy themselves. But since the restaurant was meant to be a home for all Charlestonians, they also created a quieter, more formal dining room called the Perdita's room. The space was a bit more peaceful and reserved, with big wooden columns and pastel walls. With the historic reputation of Perdita's, it was smart to pay homage to the previous restaurant and provide a place for some of the older regulars to enjoy.

Carolina's concept was a bit of a leap for the owners, since it took a step away from traditional Charleston expectations. Restaurateur Dick Elliott said in 2013, "It was a New York–style restaurant. It was hip…. It was a melding of contemporary and Charleston influences. It was the place to be."[196] When Meier was asked if he felt the restaurant was modern, he was a bit reluctant, replying, "Eh, like California five years before." Regardless of the slower evolution of trends down South, it was certainly modern for Charleston.

The restaurant was a hit. In fact, it was *the* place to be seen. Managing to provide excellent service and food without being pretentious, Carolina's drew in a wide variety of customers. People would relax in jeans with a hamburger or sit in a suit with a veal chop. It was anything and everything in between. Even the waiters were making so much money that no one wanted to leave. In fact, Frank Jarrell couldn't help but give the restaurant his highest remarks. He said Carolina's "may well be the best restaurant I've visited in Charleston. Period."[197]

The menu was vast, with around forty options before even hearing the specials. Maybe that's why another local food critic, Jane Kronsberg, called it "the forerunner of the California/Southwestern/Cajun/Southern style cuisine (I call it Nouvelle American) which has become so popular lately."[198] The soups were fantastic, including onion and black bean, but Jarrell said it was worth going for the salad alone, which was topped with Clemson bleu cheese. The variety continued, from Jamaican jerk pork tenderloin to blackened sea scallops with Cajun hollandaise to sautéed Carolina crab cakes. It was also a wise choice to end a meal with a pecan brittle basket filled with ice cream and fruit coulis. Chef Rose Durden's menu was approachable fine dining, and the word *innovative* was used repeatedly.

Carolina's advertisement from
1998. *From Charleston Place, 1998.*

It wasn't just the Perdita's room that carried the traditions of the past. Carolina's menu also kept classic items such as the Fruits de la Mer and shrimp Remick. "I am certain that the Perdita ghosts are most joyful that the tradition of fine dining is being carried on in their old location," Jane Kronsberg wrote in 1991.[199]

The restaurant eventually changed owners three separate times before finally closing in 2014. The last owner, Joe Meloy, explained that he just couldn't commit to another long-term lease, especially as the trend of restaurants had moved from along East Bay to Upper King Street. Tucked away on Exchange Street, Carolina's had become easy to overlook—the run of a long-loved restaurant in Charleston had completed its course. Perhaps the recent occupancy of the building speaks to the permanence of the culinary scene's move farther up the peninsula, since it was not another restaurant that took over but Cirque Salon Studios. The new owners still pay homage to the gathering place that was Carolina's, proudly displaying the restaurant's original sign in the foyer.

4

A Renewed Focus on Local Offerings

When Chef Louis Osteen opened Louis's Charleston Grill in the Omni Hotel in 1989, it garnered the sort of attention Charleston needed to continue to build its reputation as a culinary epicenter. Osteen was considered "one of the most gifted chefs in America" and took the opportunity to showcase southern cooking.[200] This focus on local ingredients became increasingly popular around town, especially following the devastation and rebuilding process from Hurricane Hugo. After all, Charleston's coastal location offers plenty of fresh seafood and produce.

Growth in Charleston continued with that focus on local culture, cuisine and preservation. Hotels like the Courtyard by Marriott and Embassy Suites opened downtown, which offered more rooms for the booming tourism industry. Potential business owners saw Charleston as an opportunity to make an easy dollar, and restaurants began popping up all over the peninsula. However, this growth wasn't without consequences, and by 1998, the competition downtown was fierce. Since most of these restaurants were independently owned (as opposed to the national average of 60 percent chain ownership of restaurants),[201] many had to carefully consider the competition for a finite number of customers and rising costs of business ownership.

Things were on such an upswing that a gung-ho group decided Charleston had the potential to host its own food and wine festival to rival other big cities. The group managed to pull off the grand idea when the Wine and Food Festival premiered in March 2006. With our place on the culinary map all but solidified, development continued to march forward. The restaurant boom had arrived.

When revitalization eventually hit Upper King Street, the impacts were felt directly by restaurant owners. Rising rent, gentrification and a change in tourist foot traffic all created a new scene north of Calhoun Street. Just like the conundrum of Pete's Restaurant after Hurricane Hugo, many people wondered if they should get out of their investments quickly or hold out for improvements in the surrounding areas. Unfortunately, all of this change led to a loss of a few beloved restaurants.

ALICE'S RESTAURANT

Alice Warren is, quite frankly, a soul food legend in Charleston. Her career in the restaurant industry began in 1967, when she worked at the Ladson House and eventually took over the position of manager when owner Eddie Ladson had to take a step back. Her endless work ethic and genuine personality took her far in the industry, and she learned quite a bit from watching and working with Eddie Ladson, her mentor and one of her biggest supporters. "No matter how far you go, you've got to start somewhere, and Mr. Ladson gave me my start. I'll never forget him," Alice said about Ladson in an interview in 1997.[202] She worked at the Ladson House until it closed in 1985.

A friend and patron of the Ladson House, Price Witaker, opened a restaurant at the corner of King and Cleveland Streets in 1986, offering Alice not only the job of manager and chief cook but also the namesake. It would be called Alice's Restaurant. "I named the restaurant after Alice because if you mention her name to people that know, they know she's a great cook," Price said in an interview in 1987.[203]

Alice's Restaurant remained until 1989, when Hurricane Hugo wiped out the building. Not one to let something like a hurricane stop her, Alice charged on to find a new location. In 1990, she was able to open Alice's Southern Vittles in a little spot on Meeting Street. Eventually faced with a fairly good problem to have, Alice needed a bigger building to match her growing success and soul food popularity. An auto parts store at 468 King Street turned into the home of Alice's Fine Foods and Southern Cooking in October 1994.

Her cooking style was always reflected in her menus—somewhere in the categories of southern, homestyle or Sunday dinner any day of the week. Alice served up fried chicken, ox tails, red rice, collard greens, corn bread, macaroni and cheese, succotash and sweet tea. Dessert included banana pudding and homemade cakes, and guests could eat at the buffet or take carryout.

Just like many of the best restaurants, Alice's wasn't only about the food—people came for the atmosphere, as well. For example, her Sunday Jazz Brunch managed to bring just about everyone in the community together. So much so that nearby businesses were motivated to open later hours on Sunday afternoons to cater to the crowd rolling out of her restaurant.

Unfortunately, the height of her business didn't last forever, especially with the economic turnaround on Upper King Street leading to higher rents. While Alice's restaurant closed, it's not surprising that she didn't stop cooking. In fact, she can be found hard at work at the restaurant My Three Sons in North Charleston.

ERNIE'S RESTAURANT

At 64 Spring Street, Ernie's had been delivering soul food since 1977. While Ernie Kinloch's name happened to be on the restaurant, it was his sisters who ran the kitchen. Their family-run business made the customers feel like family.

The signature dish at Ernie's was lima beans—the kind cooked with pig tails and neck bones. But if beans weren't a personal favorite, customers could also find turkey necks, baked barbecue ribs, hoppin' John, okra soup served over rice, smothered oxtail, red rice and fish or black-eyed peas. It was the very best kind of comfort food that attracted a solid following, even without advertising. It was tucked far enough away on Spring Street that locals felt lucky to know about it. The regulars knew what was available and didn't have to rely on a menu.

Ernie's served hundreds of people every day, especially with their popular takeout business. This included customers from the local hospitals, colleges and businesses nearby, who relied on Ernie's for lunch. While it mostly flew under the radar, Ernie's appeared on the Charleston Wine and Food Festival soul food tour in 2012, which afforded them more than a few new loyal customers. An interview with nephew Antuan Kinloch in 2013 added insight to the small space's experience with the tour, as he explained, "This place was packed. We were so busy, I was second guessing myself whether we should have done this."[204]

Despite the popularity, the business needed to close for renovations and hoped to reopen, but citing Ernie's sister's illness, they were forced to remain closed. It's also not a stretch to blame the rising rents in a quickly gentrified area of town as an impact on business. After nearly forty years, Ernie's closed up shop in 2013, and after extensive renovations, Josephine Wine Bar opened in its place in 2018.

LATASHA'S TASTE OF NEW ORLEANS

Robert Pinckney was born in New Orleans but came to South Carolina to open the first authentic Creole restaurant in the state. He had many successes over the years as a restaurant owner and chef, opening eight different restaurants in the area that were all named after his daughter, LaTasha.

Pinckney's restaurant on the corner of Cannon and Coming Streets opened in 1994, with plenty of red rice and beans, shrimp creole, blackened steak and fish or po'boy sandwiches to choose from. There were also specialty items such as seafood à la LaTasha, which included crab, shrimp, scallops, cheese and breadcrumbs.[205]

The restaurant was still considered a bit out of the way in the mid-1990s, even though it was just two blocks off King Street. Pinckney relied on a local crowd to keep his business going and said, "To tell you the truth, I prefer my locals and I tell them that," in an interview in 1998. He continued, "I'm not saying I don't want the tourist business, but I definitely want locals. It's steadier business."[206]

That local business kept his lunch hour busy, but he had a harder time filling the dinner hours. "We had a strong lunch crowd, but lunch couldn't pay the rent,"[207] said owner Robert Pinkney after the restaurant finally closed in 2002. The spot is now home to the Cannon Street location of Five Loaves Cafe.

FISH

While many restaurants were on their way out with the changes on Upper King Street, other restaurateurs were looking to take a chance on investing in the area. Patrick Properties Hospitality Group was one of those investors, with a keen eye for restoration and preservation. In the late '90s, the group purchased the historic American Theater and William Aiken house and took a gamble on a group of vacant buildings in the 400 block of King Street.[208] With foresight into the future of the area, they felt it was the perfect spot for a restaurant.

Fish opened in 2000, in an era when there still wasn't much around them. Perhaps beacons for the scene of future culinary powerhouses, they set up shop among bars at the time. The location was an old Charleston single house from 1837. Several previous owners had applied to have the building demolished due to its rundown state, but the Board of Architectural Review denied those requests in order to save the historic site.[209] Patrick Properties revamped the neglected space into a beautiful restaurant focused on quality local ingredients.

Chef Nico Romo came on board in 2007 and started by throwing away all of the dishes in the building. He wanted to start anew, with a focus on a more casual French bistro atmosphere. The French native had honed his impeccable talent in his home country before studying under French master chefs in Memphis and Atlanta. Romo eventually earned the prestigious title himself—the youngest person to do so.[210]

The restaurant was renovated in 2008, a sign of a business ever adapting to the changing environment, as well as its trust in their young, ambitious new chef. Nico added an Asian flair to his French cuisine, with a dim sum menu and cheese plates. Fish's happy hour was legendary on King Street, and its Bastille celebrations extended from Marion Square.

Nico Romo left in 2016 to open his own restaurant in Mount Pleasant, which left an opening for new chef David Schuttenberg. When Fish closed in 2017, the group had its eye on continued change. While many mourned the loss of an Upper King staple, the group remained in the building to open its new concept, Parcel 32.

LANA

The first version of Lana was known as Cafe Lana, and it resided at 30 Cumberland Street from 2000 to 2004. Opened by Chef Drazen Romic, a native of Bosnia, Lana was always one of those well-kept local secrets as a spot for lunch. The café served sandwiches, soups and salads, as well as tapas and pastas for dinner. With a European flair, the cooks worked out of a tiny, yet somehow still efficient, kitchen. The business, named for Romic's daughter, was forced out when the building owner decided to head in a different direction with the space. Other local businesses, such as Cumberland's Pub and Grill and Theatre 99, were displaced by the same decision. This sad chain of events was a sign of the times for raising rents.

The most affordable property options were north of Calhoun Street, which was still a relative risk in the early 2000s. But with Robert Stehling's Hominy Grill paving the way, there was a sense of development and hope for the area. Lana took over a space on the corner of Rutledge and Cannon in 2005, after spending months on a heavy-handed renovation. The owners had to rip up and repour concrete floors themselves as they attempted to remove the traces of the previous convenience store with questionable offerings. They had a vision within the mess to create a fresh start.

Drazen Romic had partnered with Chef John Ondo for Lana's reimagining, which was then named Lana's Restaurant and Bar. The space was still small and cozy, but it somehow felt large in comparison to its original space. The goal was to create a neighborhood spot for Italian food, such as gnocchi, risotto and local fish—all with a bit of Mediterranean flair. Drazen's vinaigrette from the Cafe Lana days remained on the menu, and a pear and gorgonzola salad developed quite the following. Chef John Ondo stated in an interview on the restaurant's ten-year anniversary that they received threats of bricks through windows from little old ladies when the salad was briefly removed from the menu.[211]

The area of Cannonborough continued to grow, and the neighborhood awakened to a new identity. Businesses on Upper King had continued to increase, while MUSC and the College of Charleston expanded. For a while, dinners in the area were still less popular. According to Ondo, someone's mother once said she'd only come to his restaurant for lunch, as she felt the area was too questionable for dinner service. In all fairness, Limehouse would deliver the restaurant's produce at 7:30 in the morning, and by 8:00, half of it would be missing. They also had a few bikes stolen, but Ondo noted that the vandalism in the area eventually shifted from graffiti to poor, destructive decisions by drunk college students. Luckily, Ondo quickly found a friend across the street in Robert Stehling, calling him "the best neighbor a guy could ask for." Not only did they help each other out, but their successful businesses also helped evolve the area around them.

The effort to become so successful came with a price, which included sixty-plus-hour workweeks. Beyond that, as a business owner, Ondo never really got to be off duty. In fact, he recalled being on vacation in Italy, when he got a call that his sous chef had walked out during service. In vacation photos that he might not want to relive, his wife had inadvertently captured the sharp contrast before and after receiving the frustrating news halfway across the world. The offer from Perig Goulet to buy the business in 2017 marked the end of Lana.

Even though the restaurant had been Ondo's blood, sweat and tears, he admits it was a relief to close. In fact, for the first time in thirteen years, he was able to go on a real vacation without the possibility of interruption. It probably didn't hurt knowing that the space would be in the good hands of his friend, Goulet. The two had known each other for nearly twenty-five years and had worked together at Il Cortile Del Re, an Italian restaurant on lower King Street, which opened in 1996 and ran for eighteen years.

Goulet wasn't a novice to restaurant ownership in Charleston either, as he had opened his own place, La Fourchette, back in 2005. In a short amount of time, chef and owner Goulet managed to make quite an impression with the French Bistro on King Street, which was supplied with recipes from his native Brittany.

The candlelit setting at La Fourchette offered legendary hand-cut pommes frites that were double fried in duck fat. Live accordion music added to the ambiance, and exposed brick and a black-and-white floor transformed guests to a different place. But there was absolutely no ketchup for those frites, only mayonnaise and Dijon mustard dipping sauce.

In 2011, La Fourchette was even named one of the three best French bistros in North America by the Cooking Channel's show *Unique Eats*.[212] The menu offered staples for a French bistro, which included homemade pâté, steamed mussels with a broth for dipping baguettes and cassoulet with meat and white beans. A perfect ending to a meal would include the profiteroles filled with vanilla ice cream and topped with chocolate sauce. The food consisted of quality ingredients with perfect presentation.

Goulet eventually sold his restaurant space on King Street to Hall Hospitality Group and stated, "I always welcome change and after eight years it's time for me to relax a bit and take a vacation."[213] So, when Goulet announced the opening of Goulette Rotisserie and Grill in the old Lana space, Charleston welcomed him back with open arms.

At the time Lana closed, Ondo had already lined up a consulting job for the casual Greek restaurant Kairos in Mount Pleasant. A few of the recipes had even been tested at Lana before the closure. The position evolved and he became an operating partner of the business, which eventually opened a second location in West Ashley.

Looking for a bit of a change, Ondo is now working at a resort on Kiawah Island, running two restaurants and a banquet. But don't expect his foray back into the restaurant scene to ignite a desire to return to restaurant ownership. He's already known the stress of being a chef and business owner. When asked if he sees himself opening a restaurant in the future, Ondo replied with a simple and emphatic, "No."

MERCATO

While the restaurant scene was nothing short of dynamic on Upper King Street, transitions were happening in the Lower Peninsula as well. The building at 102 North Market Street seems ideal for a restaurant, especially since it's smack dab in the middle of the City Market. Sure, locals tend to shy away from the crowded tourist area with limited parking, but heavy foot traffic would still bring people right to the front door.

With a press release announcement, the team behind the Planters Inn reunited to open an Italian eatery in the space in 2006. This included Hank Holliday, owner of Hank's Seafood, as well as his partners, Steve and Kat Varn. They also snagged Jacques Larson to be the head chef of Hank's fourth restaurant.

The menu focused on Italian dishes, without forgetting the classic Lowcountry flair that tourists would search for within the market area. "Witness gamberoni locali e polenta, local shrimp with house-made pancetta and tomatoes over Anson Mills polenta and ravioli di Lowcountry, stuffed with collard greens and ham hocks, served in a sour broth," the press release announced.[214]

The decor was rich, including Venetian plaster walls, Italian leather on the banquette chairs and an Italian chandelier from the 1950s. Chef Larson described the challenges of such a distinct interior during an interview in 2014 with *Eater Charleston*: "With Mercato, I really wanted everything to be under twenty dollars, but Hank ended up adding Murano glass and Venetian plaster to the restaurant."[215] This higher overhead increased the price point of the menu to a level where people were paying a lot of money for pasta dishes, especially in a recession.

When water damage was discovered during the holiday season in 2013, they closed the restaurant with little notice—a surprise to the community and their employees. However, in this closure they also decided to go in a completely new direction with the space, shifting from Italian to French cuisine. Another press release was issued in 2014, stating they would "significantly remodel and reposition the restaurant" and reopen months later with the new concept.[216]

Brasserie Gigi opened in Mercato's space in April 2014. Frank McMahon became the executive chef, and the restaurant was named for his wife, Gigi. McMahon said, "We're not reinventing the wheel here. It's all recognizable French stuff, but on the Market, we have a broad range of people that we're appealing to."[217] The menu included items such as shrimp Provençale and duck confit, as well as a raw bar with oysters and clams.

Hanna Raskin's review in the *Post and Courier* in 2014 found the new French restaurant to be just the right level of comfort to appeal to the tourist scene in the market area—the sort of idyllic French design we all want to imagine ourselves in. McMahon's extensive seafood experience was also evident in Raskin's review, as she enjoyed the grilled squid salad, monkfish bourride and shrimp Provençale. A testament to the prejudice of its address, Raskin cautioned, "It would be a shame if local eaters held the restaurant's location and welcoming demeanor against it."[218]

In all fairness, it is easy to vilify a part of town simply based on its current reputation. It's the same reason I acknowledge that I'm too old to tolerate the drunken chaos of some parts of Upper King Street on a Saturday night. But even I found myself braving the City Market to visit Brasserie Gigi a few times during its tenure. In fact, my husband and I dined there on New Year's Eve in 2015, just two days before they announced their closure. There wasn't a hint that the end was near; the food and drinks were perfect, while the ambiance remained warm and inviting.

When the news was eventually announced, most people were surprised, but none more than the staff, who had no official warning about the closure. Almost in a strange sense of déjà vu, the space closed once again right after the holiday season. Sure, there had to have been a few whispers, since the restaurant was a part of Hank Holliday's properties that were sold to an investment firm out of Ohio in December of that year. Phillip Cotchen, the former manager, stated that contractors had been looking at the third floor of Brasserie Gigi to possibly turn it into additional suites for the Planters Inn, but there had been no real cause for concern.

The staff was rightfully emotional about the closure. As a close-knit group of people, the one-two punch of losing a work family and a source of income was painful. Was history simply doomed to repeat itself in this location? Logistically speaking, there were challenges with the space operating as a restaurant. For starters, the large space required quite a bit of overhead to heat, light and cool down. And as one can imagine, historic property downtown isn't always the most energy efficient. The second-floor space wasn't used much for seating other than on busy weekend nights. And with a kitchen on the second floor, it wasn't fun to be a member of the support staff running up and down stairs all evening long.

So, the space sat unused, with many people wondering if another restaurant would even give it a try after the issues of previous attempts. Alas, a few months later the space reopened—as a souvenir T-shirt shop called the Black Dog. The company does have ties to a restaurant and tavern in Massachusetts, but that seems to be where the culinary connection ends. With the bar now a checkout counter and liquor bottles replaced with stacks of neatly folded T-shirts, the tourist scene appears to prevail on Market Street.

CYPRESS

Most people in the restaurant industry aren't surprised when a restaurant closes—it's just the nature of the business. However, some places simply feel more rooted than others, and Cypress was one of those restaurants.

When it opened in 2001, Cypress was the last addition to Hospitality Management Group's collection of restaurants, which included Magnolia's and Blossom, all along the same block on East Bay Street. In a building that dates back to 1834, what was once office space for a shipping line became a modern fine dining space. The decor was a perfect mix of old and new—casual yet sophisticated. Plus, the five-dollar burger deal on Mondays always brought an eclectic crowd. It was the kind of place someone could sneak a picture of Bill Murray after work, as long as they remembered to turn off their flash.

Executive chef Craig Deihl was nominated for a James Beard award three times, and his leadership was crucial to the success of the restaurant. Deihl was well known for his charcuterie and helped develop Artisan Meat Share, which closed shortly after Cypress. Deihl had worked in the family of restaurants for more than twenty years, getting his start as the sous chef at Magnolia's. He found success in the large space and even crafted his own cookbook, *Cypress: A Lowcountry Grille*. When Cypress closed, those around the city were highly anticipating his next venture, which unfortunately took him out of the state to North Carolina.

The owners might not have had to mourn for too long, since the building was sold shortly after for an impressive closing price of $6.65 million.[219] A new fine dining restaurant called Tradd's quickly took its place and opened in 2018. The changeover goes to show that regardless of the memories we form, a restaurant is still a business and things can change based on factors both in and out of an owner's control. In a city like Charleston, changes in tourist habits, development of land, parking availability and rising rent costs continue to dramatically impact the restaurant scene.

DIXIE SUPPLY BAKERY AND CAFE

The story of Dixie Supply Bakery and Cafe doesn't begin when it opened in 2007 but instead back in 1984, when Kris Holmes decided her job as a collection supervisor at Sears, Roebuck and Company wasn't as fulfilling as she'd hoped. Kris said in an interview in 1990, "I wanted to give something back to the community and spend more time with my kids. Working with a large corporation, I didn't have the opportunity to do that."[220] With a leap of faith, she took over Terrible Tom's Bakery in the market area when the original owner decided to retire. She ended up putting in a lot more hours than her corporate job, but the flexibility was welcomed.

Any spare moment Holmes could rustle up seemed to be occupied by her active role in the community. She eventually become the president of the Market Area Merchants Association and took charge after Hugo devastated the market and her own shop. "These merchants are self-motivated individuals who won't let a little thing like Hugo get in their way," she said while cleaning up the debris and refusing to be held back.[221]

When she closed up Terrible Tom's in 1993, she traveled around the United States and abroad with her husband, Allen. They took the opportunity to soak in the sites, but they also learned new recipes and techniques to take along with them. While they explored the world, Charleston worked its magnetic magic to eventually bring them back.

In 2007, Kris and Allen opened Dixie Supply Bakery and Cafe on State Street right next to the famous Li'l Cricket convenience store. It was unpretentious and focused on good food and good service. Zeroing in on a breakfast choice was difficult with options like stone ground shrimp and grits, croissant French toast and, of course, Kris's famous tomato pie with heirloom tomatoes and an herbed pie crust. They attracted locals who knew the value and caliber of the food served out of that little store front, as well as the attention of Guy Fieri from *Diners, Drive-ins, and Dives* in 2012.

When Kris unexpectedly passed away in late 2016, the community lost not only Dixie Supply Bakery and Cafe, but also a passionate business owner and community leader. However, shortly after the closure, the space

Dixie Soul Cafe has closed in the space that once housed Dixie Supply Bakery and Cafe. *From the author.*

reopened as Dixie Soul Cafe. Similar in name to its predecessor, many guests thought that it was the same restaurant. As seen in similar stories, perhaps being compared to what once was is a bit more of a curse than a blessing. Many Yelp reviewers pointed out that they missed the "old" Dixie, and the space eventually closed once again.

The closure of Dixie Supply Bakery and Cafe and the subsequent Dixie Soul Cafe warrants the question: Can you re-create the magic of a lost restaurant? Some, like those over at Harold's Cabin, have excelled at reimagining the nostalgia, while others find that living up to the public's standards of the way things used to be is incredibly challenging. But change, even when simply suggested or assumed, can be difficult to stomach.

When Charleston restaurateur Brent Petterson partnered with Wes Denney to create Brown Dog Deli, his space that was long known as Brent's on Broad underwent a bit of a transformation. While Petterson was still very much a part of the restaurant, the regular lunch crowd was hesitant to return upon the relaunch, thinking Denney might have chased Petterson away. Petterson was surprised by the response, wondering, "Why wouldn't they give him a chance?"

In all fairness, we often associate our favorite restaurants with a sense of loyalty, friendship and routine. I still haven't brought myself to try the restaurant that took over my favorite Sunday brunch spot, and Petterson's perspective made me realize I might be harboring an unfounded animosity toward a business I don't even know. But maybe these changes are simply a painful reminder of what was lost, since the memory of what was is often a lot more idyllic than the reality of what is.

5

The Future of Charleston's Restaurants

Charleston, in all of its historic glory, continues to change, whether it wants to or not. Even in the months of writing this book, restaurants around town continued to close and open and close. While some were surprising due to their longevity, we've all sort of come to expect these happenings as a way of life. People can tell when a dining room isn't filling up like it used to, when a menu keeps changing or when the quality no longer lives up to its former glory. However, some closures still feel abrupt—like a carpet being yanked from below. An overnight shutter or a place that decides not to reopen after a "winter renovation" still feels a bit more gut wrenching.

John Ondo decided to close Lana abruptly but only because there's no real correct way to close a business. Give people a heads up and the support staff might quit, or worse, just start stealing from the place. Even though it might be a hard-fought decision to close a business, Ondo said, "It brings out the spitefulness in people." Just as difficult is the moment when the staff finds out that their place of employment is closing. A group of people lose not only a friend group but also a source of income.

Locals have been speculating for decades about when Charleston would reach its restaurant limit. How can a finite amount of space mostly surrounded by water continue to grow? How can we possibly accommodate more people, more restaurants and more development? How does this growth impact tourism and what about any sense of livability? We've come a long way from that sleepy place of two o'clock dinners and a handful of choices to eat outside of home.

WHY DO RESTAURANTS CLOSE IN CHARLESTON?

Charleston remains heavily featured in the news, and as we win award after award for our enticing vacation destination, people will continue to come and expect the very best. So, just as we build more and more hotels to meet this high demand, business owners will take the opportunity to open restaurants to feed these potential customers. But in a city well known for flooding, we aren't unfamiliar with a saturation point—when too much isn't necessarily a good thing. When the choices are so abundant, you can't even feasibly support all of your favorites.

While one could easily blame the sheer number of choices, there appears to be many factors in Charleston's restaurant closures. For one, it isn't just the volume of restaurants but also the number of people who all do the same thing. When visitors have more than thirty choices for southern cuisine, it's difficult for any one place to stand out in a crowd. For this very reason I used to be guilty of lumping Cypress, Magnolia's and Blossom all together, simply because they all had the same parent company with similar menus and were all literally next door to one another.

However, on the opposite side of the coin, some specialty restaurants are too niche to capture a wide audience or price themselves too high to warrant a repeat visit anytime soon. Some restaurants reject the tourist scene to capture the locals, while others rely solely on tourist dollars and market themselves accordingly. Some owners might be focused on adapting and changing to the current trends, while others focus on their very personal passion projects. It's enough to make your head spin as a consumer, let alone as a business owner.

These owners face a multitude of unique issues in Charleston. With property values soaring, if they can't afford to buy their multimillion-dollar building, they can expect the rent to increase significantly year to year. This is not to mention the upkeep of these historic buildings that require special attention and care. Labor shortages downtown have also impacted businesses, and some owners have had to adjust their operating hours for no other reason than a lack of bodies to keep the place running. When labor is short, turnaround is high, and owners have a more difficult time guaranteeing a certain level of service necessary to stand out.

Christian Senger runs the popular local blog *Holy City Sinner* and takes on the daunting task of tracking restaurant openings and closures in the city. He has also observed the trending impact of the labor shortage in town, stating in an interview with the author, "There is lots of talk about a staffing crisis in Charleston. Many restaurants and bars are hiring, but they can't seem to find or keep enough employees—especially not good employees." He credits this issue to a mismatch in what workers can earn at a restaurant job versus the high cost of living or commuting and paying for parking downtown.

Even if someone is lucky enough to have a favorite, go-to restaurant, it's far too easy to become complacent. We think a restaurant will always be there because, well, it has always been there. Even pop-ups and food trucks can feel the pain of establishing a brick and mortar location as the sense of urgency dies down. When an old standby closes, we often have the thought, "Oh, I should have eaten there more!"—a feeling of responsibility too little, too late.

LOOKING TO THE FUTURE

With the challenges restaurant owners face in a competitive market, who will prevail? Mom and pop shops are becoming almost too expensive to open, maintain, staff and market. It's difficult enough to get something started, let alone keep it running and succeeding. When my husband and I opened our own business in Charleston, it was just a tour company with very little overhead, considering we didn't have to rent a building. However, we were still shocked at the cost of practically everything else. At first, we laughed at the absurd idea of paying thousands of dollars for a few inches of advertising space, until we realized that was simply the going rate in a popular tourist destination. I'm sure there are restaurant owners in town who are spending tens of thousands of dollars just to keep the word out about their businesses and hoping for some sort of return on their investment. With these associated costs, it makes sense to assume that places with deeper pockets and investors might be the ones to prevail.

Phillip Cotchen, 5Church manager, reminds us not to discredit the power of good service to stand out. In a city like Charleston, Cotchen acknowledges that servers are often expected to offer more than just dinner; they are essentially a kind of tour guide, offering recommendations and helping their guests plan what to do next. Rather than stuffy, formal service, he looks toward elevating the customer experience with more personality and fewer scripted responses.

Legendary Charleston restaurateur Franz Meier seemed to echo these statements by citing the importance of service details that are often missed these days, including proper attention to water glasses or knowing a regular customer's favorite dish before they even order. Going the extra mile can help a restaurant stand out and keep people coming back.

So, what changes can we expect to see next in Charleston? If anyone knew for sure, they'd be buying up all that property before someone else could. Some people guess there will be a trend toward smaller, unique spaces that offer a reason to stand out above everyone else. Others think larger corporations might start to influence the scene due to the sheer cost of operation. Some of us might just be focused on patronizing restaurants with dedicated lots or valets, considering the fact that parking on the peninsula can be frustrating, expensive and nearly impossible some days. Regardless, the scene is bound to continue to evolve.

Conclusion

A true testament to the subjective nature of the culinary world, nearly every person I interviewed had a different answer to the question, "What restaurant do you miss the most?" In all fairness, it's pretty close to that simple "what's your favorite restaurant" question that just happens to be my Achilles' heel. Some people were able to narrow down a few specific places, while others were instantly overwhelmed with the mass of options. But my favorite and most relatable answer was from Chef John Ondo, who said, "I miss the people who ran the restaurants more than anything."

His perspective perfectly sums up the depth of the stories of these lost restaurants. It's the people behind them—the life force of owners, staff and families—that can make a business something truly special. One of the best parts of owning a food tour company was getting to know the owners and staff at some of our favorite places and truly appreciating the countless hours they spent on their menus, uniforms, decor and more. When we eat at a restaurant once, we get just a snapshot of what that owner has created, but there's so much more that lies beneath the surface. So, after reading hundreds of news articles spanning an equal number of years and hearing firsthand accounts of these iconic establishments, it's much easier to appreciate the power and importance of a simple place to eat.

I know I've been lucky enough to find myself tucked in a Charleston restaurant surrounded by friends—the air conditioning on the fritz, the wait staff desperately trying to smile through the sweat and the beer coming out a few degrees below a sweltering room temperature—and still we sat happily until that moment right before the check came. The magic of the food lifted and the realization that we were all literally stewing finally set in. That's the kind of meal you'll find in Charleston. The kind that makes you (sort of) forget that you are about to pour out of your seat or that you broke your flip-flop on a jagged cobblestone or even that the tax on your drink was about as much as the drink itself. You forgive the quirks of a city for the bounty it offers. And Charleston has a lot to offer.

Notes

Chapter 1

1. Christine Chapman, "More Than Coffee Brews in Classic Coffee Houses," *News and Courier*, November 18, 1956.
2. W.H.J. Thomas, "Permit to Demolish Building is Revoked," *News and Courier*, January 22, 1972.
3. "Aaron Burr Once Guest at Establishment That Flourished," *News and Courier*, September 22, 1941.
4. Chapman, "More Than Coffee."
5. "United States Coffee House," *Charleston Courier*, January 14, 1837.
6. *Charleston Courier*, January 25, 1837.
7. Shields, *Southern Provisions*, 112.
8. "Bachelor's Retreat—Extra Dinner," *Charleston Courier*, November 24, 1862.
9. *South Carolina Inter-State*, 3.
10. Ibid.
11. "Service Station to Replace Cafe," *News and Courier*, September 10, 1939.
12. "Business Property Buyers Revealed," *Evening Post*, June 29, 1944.
13. Basil W. Hall, "Keeping Posted," *Evening Post*, September 3, 1964.
14. "Early Experiments with Laughing Gas Conducted at 2–6 Broad Street," *News and Courier*, January 5, 1948.
15. "Welcome to Demos Brothers," *News and Courier*, October 14, 1920.

16. "Demos Brothers Dairy Lunch Service Very Popular," *Evening Post*, March 19, 1924.

17. "Demos Buys Building," *Evening Post*, January 21, 1944.

18. "Peter Demos Returns to Restaurant Business," *News and Courier*, January 5, 1944.

19. "P.P. Botzis Purchases Building at 2 Broad Street," *News and Courier*, July 2, 1958.

20. "'George' Magoulas, Proud American, Dies at Age of 65," *Evening Post*, April 2, 1947.

21. "Money Given to Uncle Sam," *Evening Post*, October 22, 1941.

22. *City Gazette*, September 17, 1803.

23. *Walsh's City Directory 1904*.

24. "Old Hotel's Columns Fall," *Evening Post*, April 30, 1960.

25. *Evening Post*, March 25, 1919.

26. Jack Roach, "'Politician's Coffee Shop' to Move...But Not Far," *Evening Post*, April 28, 1960.

27. "Timrod Inn Fire Guts Top Floor," *News and Courier*, March 7, 1936.

28. Steve Bailey, "Living with the Long Brothers' Legacy," *Post and Courier*, December 18, 2015.

29. *Evening Post*, March 19, 1924.

30. *News and Courier*, April 1, 1931.

31. *News and Courier*, February 18, 1940.

32. "Fort Sumter Hotel Closes Saturday," *Evening Post*, November 3, 1973.

33. Betty Pugh, "City's Eating Places Are Big Tourist Lore," *News and Courier*, March 25, 1953.

34. *Evening Post*, March 27, 1950.

Chapter 2

35. Moore, *Complete Charleston*, 270.

36. Charles deV. Williams, "Robertson Serves Success—Cafeteria Style," *News and Courier*, June 26, 1981.

37. Ibid.

38. "After 60 Years, Cafeteria Lines Will Come to End," *Evening Post*, August 20, 1971.

39. Jack Leland, "Tap to Be Turned on Wisdom's Fount," *Evening Post*, August 21, 1971.

40. Ibid.

41. Thomas R. Waring, "Cafeteria an Institution," *News and Courier*, August 1, 1982.

42. Williams, "Robertson Serves Success."

43. Ibid.

44. Waring, "Cafeteria an Institution."

45. Charles deV. Williams, "Cafeteria at St. Andrew's an Instant Hit," *News and Courier*, May 22, 1990.

46. "Robertson's Closing Is Charleston's Sad Loss," *Evening Post*, October 19, 1989.

47. Elsa F. McDowell, "State of the Art in Cafeterias," *News and Courier*, November 24, 1988.

48. Frank Jarrell, "Cafeteria at St. Andrew's to Reopen," *News and Courier*, April 25, 1990.

49. Pauline Sottile, "Reconsider, Please?" *News and Courier*, November 1, 1989.

50. Williams, "Cafeteria at St. Andrew's."

51. Jarrell, "Cafeteria at St. Andrew's."

52. Williams, "Cafeteria at St. Andrew's."

53. Elsa F. McDowell and Charles deV. Williams, "Fyshbyrne's Cafeteria Closes Its Doors," *Post and Courier*, July 17, 1992.

54. McDowell and Williams, "Fyshbyrne's Cafeteria."

55. Ibid.

56. "Harold's Cabin Becomes Emporium from Log Cabin," *News and Courier*, September 6, 1953.

57. Ibid.

58. "Harold Jacobs on the Move," *News and Courier*, February 18, 1979.

59. Ann Burger, "Chicken Magnolia Pioneer Divulges His Secret," *Post and Courier*, September 29, 1996.

60. F. Marion Brabham, "An Open Letter to All Charlestonians," *News and Courier*, October 9, 1964.

61. Edward C. Fennell, "LaBrasca's Mama's Moved to Mount Pleasant But Her Heart Remains Downtown," *News and Courier*, August 1, 1975.

62. Douglas J. Donehue, "Mama LaBrasca Will Be Missed," *News and Courier*, October 27, 1987.

63. Fennell, "LaBrasca's Mama's."

64. Frank P. Jarrell, "Entrepreneur Learns Her Lessons from Life," *News and Courier*, October 18, 1981.

65. Janson L. Cox, "Thanks to 'Mama,'" *Evening Post*, October 29, 1987.

66. "King Restaurant is Popular Place," *Evening Post*, August 22, 1922.

67. *Evening Post*, May 27, 1933.
68. Robert Moss, "From Hooch to Haute Cuisine: Fine Dining in the Lowcountry Traced Back to Illegal Liquor Trade," *Post and Courier*, December 9, 2015.
69. Ben Perrone, "How Mini-Bottles Shaped Charleston's Cocktail Culture," *Eater Charleston*, October 16, 2015, https://charleston.eater.com.
70. "Made a Little Raid," *News and Courier*, March 17, 1897.
71. "The Hasselmeyer Case," *News and Courier*, June 8, 1897.
72. Elsa M. Freeman, "Taciturn Is the Word for Henry's Owner," *News and Courier*, April 3, 1977.
73. Henry's Restaurant Menus, 1945–1977, 1308.00, Henry's Restaurant Records, South Carolina Historical Society, Charleston, SC.
74. Dorothy Byrd, "Seafood Dishes Are Popular Here, Several Choice Recipes Are Listed," *News and Courier*, April 12, 1949.
75. Freeman, "Taciturn Is the Word."
76. Menus, 1945–1977.
77. Jack Leland, "Sale of Henry's Restaurant Spells the End of an Era for Downtown," *News and Courier*, September 9, 1985.
78. Lee and Lee, *Lee Bros.*
79. Miriam Ungerer, "Charleston: A Visit to My Past," *International Review of Food and Wine*, April 1979.
80. Frank P. Jarrell, "Henry's for Dinner," *News and Courier*, June 26, 1981.
81. Ibid.
82. "The Scarlett O'Hara," *Evening Post*, October 9, 1973.
83. "Fork Restaurant, Spring and Cannon, Will Open Today," *News and Courier*, September 19, 1951.
84. Keith Schneider, "Drive-Ins," *News and Courier*, October 3, 1980.
85. Thomas R. Waring, "Mama Kate's 48 Years in Restaurant Trade," *News and Courier*, July 8, 1984.
86. Schneider, "Drive-Ins."
87. *Evening Post*, August 16, 1947.
88. Edward C. Fennell, "Lempesis Leaving Pete's after 26 Years at Eatery," *News and Courier*, August 16, 1986.
89. Ibid.
90. Kerri Morgan, "Reclaiming Upper King," *News and Courier*, February 5, 1990.
91. Connie Hawkins, "Putting on the Grits," *News and Courier*, January 10, 1990.
92. David MacDougall, "Electrical Fire Damages Goodie House Restaurant," *Post and Courier*, December 3, 1992.

93. Emily Abedon, "Restaurant Serves Up Last Aeals as Doors Close to Customers," *Post and Courier*, December 15, 1996.

94. Isabella G. Leland, "Charleston Flavored She-Crab Soup," *News and Courier*, July 27, 1958.

95. Herb Frazier, "Secret Made Soup by Deas Special," *Evening Post*, August 10, 1989.

96. Jane Kronsberg, "Colony House an Old Standby," *Post and Courier*, December 26, 1991.

97. Teresa Taylor, "Decades of Dining: Charleston Menus from Past Reflect Changing Palates, but Love of Seafood Remains a Constant," *Post and Courier*, October 4, 2011, https://www.postandcourier.com.

98. "The Judges Have Decided!" *News and Courier*, October 9, 1953.

99. "We're Moving Soon," *Evening Post*, November 7, 1959.

100. Lentz, *Great Charleston*, 48.

101. Ibid.

102. Erin Perkins, "The Colony House Was Charleston's Standby For Almost 40 Years," *Eater Charleston*, January 29, 2015, https://charleston.eater.com.

103. Angel Postell, "An Interview with Charleston Culinary Legend Robert Dickson," *Daily Meal*, February 19, 2016, https://www.thedailymeal.com.

104. Surber, *Greater Charleston Menu*.

105. Teresa Taylor, "How Charleston Became a Fine-Dining Destination," *Post and Courier*, March 2, 2010, https://www.postandcourier.com.

106. Erin Perkins, "20 Years for Slightly North of Broad," *Eater Charleston*, December 9, 2013, https://charleston.eater.com.

107. Perkins, "20 Years."

108. Sybil Fix, "Colony House Closes; Owners Begin Anew," *Post and Courier*, November 29, 1993.

109. Ibid.

110. Basil Hall, "Keeping Posted," *Evening Post*, February 23, 1968.

111. Karen Amrhine, "At Perdita's Food Complements Elegant Setting," *News and Courier*, October 19, 1974.

112. "Perdita's Wins Holiday Dining Award," *Evening Post*, June 21, 1957.

113. "$50,000 Expansion Planned by Perdita's," *News and Courier*, March 29, 1967.

114. Hall, "Keeping Posted."

115. *Evening Post*, January 25, 1968.

116. Frank P. Jarrell, "Fare Taste," *News and Courier*, January 26, 1979.

117. Frank P. Jarrell, "Charleston Restaurants," *News and Courier*, April 3, 1979.

118. Frank P. Jarrell, "Dining Truly Fine at Carolina's," *News and Courier*, April 27, 1989.

119. Jimmy Cornelison, "Just 'Gus,'" *News and Courier*, April 22, 1979.

120. "Doing the Charleston," *News and Courier*, May 18, 1989.

121. Patricia B. Jones, "Restaurant a Neighborhood Fixture," *Post and Courier*, July 8, 1993.

122. Jack Leland, "Kitty's Caters to Out-to-Lunch Bunch," *News and Courier*, January 27, 1980.

123. Bobbin Huff, "Kitty's Purrs to Its Customers," *News and Courier*, July 12, 1976.

124. Thomas R. Waring, "Ladson Manager Lightens Load," *News and Courier*, March 29, 1981.

125. "New Restaurant to Open," *Evening Post*, April 20, 1963.

126. David Slade, "Councilman Has Vision for Vacant West Side Properties," *Post and Courier*, August 25, 2004.

127. Waring, "Ladson Manager."

128. Jim Young, "Albert Brooks: Learn from Others," *News and Courier*, March 16, 1982.

129. *Evening Post*, January 28, 1967.

130. "Doing the Charleston," *News and Courier*, July 17, 1970.

131. Warren Koon, "The Use of Opportunities," *Evening Post*, January 25, 1967.

132. "Seamen's Chapel on Waterfront," *News and Courier*, December 12, 1914.

133. "New Role Slated for Old Chapel," *News and Courier*, August 5, 1966.

134. Craig Claiborne, "Charleston Dining, Brown Bags in Tow," *News and Courier*, November 2, 1967.

135. Frank P. Jarrell, "To Market, to Market," *News and Courier*, November 21, 1980.

136. "Barge to Become Restaurant," *News and Courier*, September 2, 1973.

137. "Barge Hits Floating Restaurant," *Evening Post*, September 24, 1975.

138. "Floating Restaurant Sinks," *News and Courier*, January 29, 1979.

139. "Corps Ties Off Sunken Restaurant," *News and Courier*, February 2, 1979.

140. Fred Rigsbee, "Contract Let for Removal of Scarlett O'Hara," *Evening Post*, Mart 13, 1979.

Chapter 3

141. Elsa Freeman, "Good Food and Music Combine at Robert's," *News and Courier*, November 6, 1976.

142. Dora Ann Reaves, "Festival of the Arts Planned," *Evening Post*, March 25, 1976.

143. Frank P. Jarrell, "Charleston Restaurants: In the Midst of a Boom," *News and Courier*, August 21, 1980.

144. Ibid.

145. Sandy Summer, "Celebrated Chef Doesn't Like the Label of 'Gourmet Cook,'" *News and Courier*, October 30, 1977.

146. Ibid.

147. Dickson, *Robert's Dinner for Six*.

148. Frank Jarrell, "Dining at Robert's," *News and Courier*, January 4, 1980.

149. James A. Martin, "Sing for Your Supper," *News and Courier*, May 14, 1982.

150. Warren Wise, "Musical Feast to End—Singing Chef at Robert's Hanging Up Hat after Decades on Charleston Scene," *Post and Courier*, October 17, 2009.

151. Cynthia Kahn, "Robert's Restaurant Staging a Comeback," *Post and Courier*, April 2, 1998.

152. John McDermott, "Downtown Restaurant Growth May Be Reaching Its Limit," *Post and Courier*, May 25, 1998.

153. Jeff Allen, "After 33 Years, Robert Dickson Hangs Up His Toque," *Charleston City Paper*, February 17, 2010, https://www.charlestoncitypaper.com.

154. Wise, "Musical Feast."

155. Allen, "After 33 Years"; Christine W. Randall, "Restaurants in Review: Robert's of Charleston," *News and Courier*, March 8, 1985.

156. R.T. Perry, "Marianne Charleston's Newest French Restaurant," *News and Courier*, December 10, 1977.

157. Ibid.

158. Frank P. Jarrell, "Pass the Crepes and Quiche Lorraine—Ethnic Restaurants Give People a Choice," *Evening Post*, July 13, 1982.

159. Edward C. Fennell, "Restaurant Operator, City Gearing for a Showdown," *News and Courier*, June 24, 1982.

160. John P. McDermott, "Marianne Replaced by Sticky Fingers," *Post and Courier*, January 5, 1996.

161. *Post and Courier*, January 8, 1996.

162. Eleanor Flagler, "Speeches, Smiles Abound as Market Square Opens," *News and Courier*, April 23, 1977.

163. Elsa M. Freeman, "Choices Abound at the Gourmetisserie," *News and Courier*, June 11, 1977.

164. Ibid.

165. "A Guide to Dining Out," *Post and Courier*, May 4, 1989.

166. *On the Towne*, 39.

167. Robert Behre, "New Hotel, Shops Approved for Market Street," *Post and Courier*, August 27, 1999.

168. Frank P. Jarrell, "Dinner at San Miguel's," *News and Courier*, February 15, 1980.

169. Willard Stron, "Yuppie Locales to See and Be Seen," *News and Courier*, July 16, 1988.

170. Lawrence Stratton, "South Carolina's Own Edwin McCain Comes Full Circle," *Post and Courier*, May 17, 2012.

171. Thomas R. Waring, "Welshman Picks Charleston," *News and Courier*, May 13, 1979.

172. Clay Barbour, "Tommy Condon: Charleston Restaurateur Has Made Most of Life's Opportunities," *Post and Courier*, March 15, 2003.

173. Charles Williams, "Condon Brothers Have Learned from Failures as Well as Success," *Post and Courier*, October 30, 2000.

174. Robert P. Stockton, "Old Saloon Becomes Restaurant," *News and Courier*, May 16, 1977.

175. Kinsey Gidick, "After 37 Years, Norm's Has Closed Making Way for Smith Street Pizza," *Charleston City Paper*, February 13, 2017, https://www.charlestoncitypaper.com.

176. "Visitors Get Look at New Restaurant," *Evening Post*, April 18, 1980.

177. Connie Hawkins, "All in Good Taste," *Post and Courier*, Feb 24, 1993.

178. James A. Martin, "Food Is to Be Experienced, French Restaurateur Believes," *News and Courier*, November 22, 1983.

179. Frank P. Jarrell, "Tavern Historique One of City's Newest Restaurants," *News and Courier*, May 27, 1983.

180. Ibid.

181. Frank P. Jarrell, "Restaurant Million—Top-Flight Dining in Historic Tavern," *News and Courier*, February 2, 1989.

182. Frank P. Jarrell, "Fare Taste Readers Bite Back," *News and Courier*, June 24, 1983.

183. Jarrell, "Fare Taste."

184. Christine W. Randall, "Restaurants in Review—Philippe Million," *News and Courier*, April 26, 1985.

185. Bill Thompson, "Restaurant's Chef Now Its Owner," *News and Courier*, October 30, 1988.

186. Frank P. Jarrell, "Restaurant Million," *News and Courier*, February 2, 1989.

187. Larry Townsend, "Walk It to Get the 'Feel' of Charleston," *Chicago Tribune*, March 17, 1991.

188. Perkins, "20 Years."

189. Frank P. Jarrell, "Dining Out on Upswing," *News and Courier*, January 12, 1990.

190. "Two Great Restaurants Now Opened," *News and Courier*, March 4, 1990.

191. John P. McDermott, "Historic 2 Unity Alley Sells Fast," *Post and Courier*, October 5, 1996.

192. John P. McDermott, "1999 a Year of Expansion for the Family-Owned Grocery Chain," *Post and Courier*, January 25, 1999.

193. Robert Behre, "Saks' Ripple Effect," *Post and Courier*, October 24, 1994.

194. McDermott, "Downtown Restaurant Growth."

195. Jack McCray, "Era Ends, Couple Awarded for Service to Jazz," *Post and Courier*, June 3, 2010.

196. Perkins, "20 Years."

197. Frank P. Jarrell, "Restaurants in Review—Carolina's," *News and Courier*, May 15, 1987.

198. Jane Kronsberg, "Ordering Isn't Easy with a Menu Like Carolina's," *Post and Courier*, October 24, 1991.

199. Ibid.

Chapter 4

200. Moore, *Complete Charleston*, 271.

201. John McDermott, "Downtown Restaurant Growth May Be Reaching Its Limit," *Post and Courier*, May 25, 1998.

202. Jeff Nichols, "Alice Warren: Restaurant Owner Can't Slow Down," *Post and Courier*, September 13, 1997.

203. Charles Francis, "Alice Warren Making the Most of Her Opportunities at Restaurant," *News and Courier*, June 11, 1987.

204. Shirley Greene, "Every Day Is Sunday at Ernie's," *Post and Courier*, April 1, 2013.

205. Patricia B. Jones, "Pinckney Opens New Restaurant," *Post and Courier*, February 3, 1994.

206. McDermott, "Downtown Restaurant."

207. Brian Hicks, "Alice Sadly Closes Doors to Popular Eatery," *Post and Courier*, October 26, 2002.

208. Kyle Stock, "Doing It Right Local Hospitality Company Builds Empire," *Post and Courier*, August 12, 2007.

209. Jim Parker, "Patrick Properties Gives New Meaning to Mom-and-Pop Developers," *Post and Courier,* September 9, 2002.

210. Rob Young, "Meet Your Master Fish's French-Born Chef Nico Romo Earns a Major Honor," *Post and Courier*, April 22, 2010.

211. Erin Perkins, "After 10 Years, Chef John Ondo Continues to Love His Work at Lana," *Eater Charleston*, April 6, 2015, https://charleston.eater.com.

212. Erin Perkins, "La Fourchette to Close This Week UPDATE: Tomorrow," *Eater Charleston*, October 14, 2013, https://charleston.eater.com.

213. Ibid.

214. "Charleston's Newest Italian Restaurant to Debut in City Market," *Charleston Visitors Bureau*, June, 2006, https://www.charlestoncvb.com.

215. Erin Perkins, "From Apathy to Elation: 5 Years in at Wild Olive [Updated]," *Eater Charleston*, March 5, 2014, https://charleston.eater.com.

216. Erin Perkins, "Mercado's Closing a Surprise to Employees," *Eater Charleston*, January 6, 2014, https://charleston.eater.com.

217. Kinsey Gidick, "Openings: Brasserie Gigi and Bistro Toulouse," *Charleston City Paper*, April 4, 2014, https://www.charlestoncitypaper.com.

218. Hanna Raskin, "Brasserie Gigi," *Post and Courier*, June 19, 2014.

219. Warren L. Wise, "Former Cypress Restaurant Building in Charleston Sells for $6.65 Million; Fleet Landing Owners to open Fine Dining Venue," *Post and Courier*, October 5, 2017.

220. Chris Sosnowski, "Owner of Terrible Tom's Bakery Is Doing 'Terrific,'" *News and Courier*, October 21, 1990.

221. Charles Francis, "Market Merchants Hit the Pluff Mud Running," *News and Courier*, October 12, 1989.

Bibliography

Print

Charleston Place. Charleston, SC: Waterfront Publishing, 1998.

Dickson, Robert. *Robert's Dinner for Six.* Charleston, SC: Tradd Street Press, 1978.

Hill's Charleston City Directory. Richmond, VA: Hill Directory Company, 1969.

Hill's Charleston City Directory. Richmond, VA: Hill Directory Company, 1972.

Historic Charleston Foundation. *The City of Charleston Tour Guide Training Manual.* Charleston, SC: City of Charleston, 2011.

Lee, Matt, and Ted Lee. *The Lee Bros. Charleston Kitchen.* New York: Clarkson Potter, 2013.

Lentz, Ginny. *The Great Charleston Catalogue: A Selective Guide to the Best, Most Unusual Restaurants, Attractions, Entertainment, Specialty Shops, and Landmarks.* Charleston, SC: Lentz Enterprises, 1983.

Moore, Margaret. *Complete Charleston: A Guide to the Architecture, History, and Gardens of Charleston.* Charleston, SC: TM Photography, 2005.

Nelsons' Charleston City Directory: Master Edition. Charleston, SC: Nelsons' Baldwin Directory Company, 1955.

On the Towne. Vol. 3. North Myrtle Beach: Himmelsbach Communications, 1984.

Shields, David S. *Southern Provisions: The Creation and Revival of a Cuisine.* Chicago: University of Chicago Press, 2015.

Surber, Larry C. *Greater Charleston Menu Guide: Second Edition.* Charleston, SC: Dynamic '76, 1980.

The South Carolina Inter-State and West Indian Exposition Official Guide. 2nd ed. Charleston, SC: Lucas-Richardson Company, 1901.

Walsh's Charleston, South Carolina 1904 City Directory. Charleston: Walsh Directory Company, 1904.

Walsh's Charleston, South Carolina 1919 City Directory. Charleston: Walsh Directory Company, 1919.

Walsh's Charleston, South Carolina 1922 City Directory. Charleston: Walsh Directory Company, 1922.

Interviews

Brent Petterson, interview by author, July 24, 2018.

Celia Cerasoli, interview by author, January 17, 2019.

Christian Senger, interview by author, April 9, 2019.

Edward Pressor, interview by author, January 15, 2019.

Franz Meier, interview by author, January 17, 2019.

Ginny Snipes, interview by author, January 22, 2019.

John Ondo, interview by author, February 4, 2019.

John Schumacher, interview by author, February 6, 2019.

Leo Chiagkouris, interview by author, January 31, 2019.

MariElena Raya, interview by author, January 23, 2019.

Phillip Cotchen, interview by author, February 2, 2019.

Robert Dickson, interview by author, January 24, 2019.

About the Author

Jessica Surface is a certified tour guide with the City of Charleston. She started Chow Down Charleston Food Tours in 2014 with her husband, Reid. It is focused on showcasing smaller, off-the-beaten-path restaurants that people have a tendency to overlook when they visit the city. In her spare time, Jessica also works as a pediatric occupational therapist and lives in Mount Pleasant, South Carolina, with her husband and two dogs, Stu and Dori.

Visit us at
www.historypress.com